Richard Baxter

Two Treatises Tending to Awaken Secure Sinners

Richard Baxter

Two Treatises Tending to Awaken Secure Sinners

ISBN/EAN: 9783337289959

Printed in Europe, USA, Canada, Australia, Japan

Cover: Foto ©Suzi / pixelio.de

More available books at **www.hansebooks.com**

TWO
TREATISES
Tending to awaken
Secure Sinners.

Viz.

1. The Terror of the Day of Judgment, from 2 *Cor.* 5. 10.

2. The Danger of slighting Christ and his Gospel, from *Matth.* 22. 5.

By *RICHARD BAXTER.*

The Gift of the Author.

LONDON,
Printed for *Jonas Luntley* at the Three Bibles in Little *Lincolns-Inn-fields.* 1696.

To the Ignorant or Careless Reader.

SEeing the Providence of God hath commanded forth these plain Discourses, I shall hope (upon Experience of his dealing in the like Cases with me) that he hath some work for them to do in the World. Who knows but they were intended for the saving of thy Soul, by opening thine Eyes, and awaking thee from thy Sin, who art now in reading of them! Be it known to thee it is the certain Truth of God, and of high Concernment to thy Soul that they treat of, and therefore require thy most sober Consideration. Thou hast in them (how weakly soever managed by me) an Advantage put into thy Hand from God, to help thee in the greatest Work in the World, even to prepare for the great approaching Judgment, and not to slight Christ and his Gospel. In the Name of God, I require thee cast not away this Advantage: Turn not away thine Ears or Heart from this warning that is sent to thee from the living God! Seeing all the World cannot keep thee from Judgment, let not all the World be able to keep thee from a speedy and serious Preparation for it. Do it presently, lest God come before thou art ready. Do it seriously, lest the Tempter over-reach thee, and thou shouldst be found among the foolish Self-deceivers when it is too late to do it better. I intreat this of thee on the behalf of thy Soul, and as thou tenderest thy everlasting Peace with God, that thou wouldest afford these Matters thy deepest Consideration. Think on them, whether they are not true and weighty: Think of them lying down and rising up. And seeing this small Book is faln into thy hands, all that I would beg of thee concerning it, is, that thou wouldst bestow now and then an Hour to read it, and read it to thy Family or Friends as well as to thy self: and as you go, consider what you read, and pray to the Lord to help it to thy Heart, and to assist thee in the Practice, that it may not rise up in Judgment against thee. If thou have not leisure at other, take now and then an Hour on the Lord's Days, or at Night to that purpose: and if any Passage, through brevity (specially near the Beginning) seem dark to thee, read it again and again, and ask the help of an Instructer, that thou mayest understand it. May it but help thee out of the Snares of Sin, and promote the saving of thy Immortal Soul, and thy Comfortable Appearance at the great Day of Christ, I have the thing which I intended and desired. The Lord open thy Heart, and accompany his Truth with the Blessing of his Spirit. Amen.

Discourse of the Terror of the Day of Judgment.

Cor. 5. 10, 11. *For we must all appear before the Judgment-Seat of Christ, that every one may receive the things done in his Body, according to that he hath done, whether it be good or bad. Knowing therefore the Terrors of the Lord, we perswade Men.*

T is not unlikely that some of those Wits that are taken more with things new than with things necessary, will marvel that I choose so common a Subject, and tell me that they all know this already. But I do it purposely upon these following Considerations. 1. Because I well know it is these common Truths that are the great and necessary things which is everlasting Happiness or Misery doth most depend upon. You may be ignorant of many Controversies and inferiour Points, without the Danger of your Souls, but so you cannot of these Fundamentals. Because it's apparent by the Lives of Men, that few know these common Truths savingly, that think they know them. 3. Because there are several Degrees of knowing the same Truths, and the best are imperfect in Degree; the principal Growth in Knowledg that we should look after, is not to know *more* Matters than we knew before, but to know *that better* and with a clearer Light and firmer Apprehension, which we darkly and slightly knew before. You may more safely be without *any* Knowledg at all of many lower Truths, than without *some farther Degree* of the Knowledg of those which you already know. 4. Besides, it is known by sad Experience, that many perish who know the Truth, for want of the Consideration of it, and making use of what they know, and so their Knowledg doth but condemn them. We have as much need therefore to teach and help you to get these Truths which you know, into your Hearts and Lives, as to tell you more. 5. And indeed, it is the Impression of these great and Master-Truths, wherein the Vitals and Essentials of God's Image upon the Soul of Man doth consist: and it is these Truths that are the very Instruments of the great Works that are to be done upon the Heart by the Spirit and our selves. In the right use of these it is that the principal Part of the Skill and holy Wisdom of a Christian doth consist; and in the diligent and constant Use of these lieth the Life and Trade of Christianity. There is nothing amiss in Mens Hearts or Lives, but is for want of sound Knowing and Believing, or well using these Fundamentals. 6. And moreover, methinks in this Choice of my Subject, I may expect this Advantage with the Hearers, that I may spare that Labour that else would be necessary for the Proof of my Doctrine: and that I may also have easier Access to your Hearts, and have a fuller Stroak at them, and with less Resistance. If I came to tell you of any thing not Common, I know not how far I might expect Belief from you. You might say, *These things are uncertain to us, or all Men are not of this Mind.* But when every Hearer confesseth the Truth of my Doctrine, and no Man can deny it, without denying Christianity it self; I hope I may expect that your Hearts should the sooner receive the Impression of this Doctrine, and the sooner yield to the Duties it directs you to, and the easier of my Text, are the Reaſon which the both of his perſwading other Men to the and his Care to approve to God his Life. They contain the Aſſertion and the Great Judgment, and one Uſe which t. It aſſureth us that judged we *muſt be*, be ſo judged, and *by whom*, and *about what Terms*, and *to what End*.

g of the Words, ſo far as is neceſſary, briefly. *We all*, both we Apoſtles that ſpel, and you that hear it, *muſt*, willing here is no avoiding it, *appear*, ſtand forth, appearance, and there have your Hearts l open, and appear as well as we. *Before it of Chriſt*, i. e. before the Redeemer of be judged by him as our Rightful Lord. even of all Mankind, which are, were, or ut Exception; *may receive*, that is, may re-nce, adjudging him to his due; and then e Execution of the Sentence, and may go with that Reward or Puniſhment that is his to the Law by which he is judged. *The his Body*, that is, the due Reward of the in his Body; or as ſome Copies read it, *er to the Body*, i. e. due to the Man, even s Soul, *according to what he hath done, whether ad*; i. e. this is the Cauſe to be tried and ner Men have done well or ill, whilſt the Fleſh, and what is due to them accor-Deeds. *Knowing therefore*, &c. *i. e.* be-erefore that theſe Things are ſo, and that Judgment of Chriſt will come, we per-become Chriſtians and live as ſuch, that n ſpeed well, when others ſhall be deſtroy-ers, *Knowing the Fear of the Lord*, that is, ion, *we perſwade Men*.

Doct. 1. There will be a Judgment. will be the Judg. *Doct.* 3. All Men sha *Doct.* 4. Men shall be then judged acc Works that they did in the Flesh, wh Evil. *Doct.* 5. The End of Judgment may receive their final Due by Sentence *Doct.* 6. The Knowledg and Considerati ble Judgment of God, should move us ai d Men to be perswaded to careful Prep

The ordinary Method for the handli ject of Judgment should be this. 1*st* what Judgment is in the General, an contain: and that is, 1. The Persons. 3. The Actions. 1. The Parties are, (ser. (2.) The Defendant. (3.) Some (4.) The Judg. 2. The Cause conta Accusation. (2.) The Defence. (3.) dence of both. (4.) And the Merit. the Cause is as it agreeth with the La 3. The judicial Actions are, I. Introd tation. 2. Compulsion, if need be. of the Accused. II. Of the Essence 1. Debate by, (1.) The Accuser. (called the Disceptation of the Cause. 2 1. Exploration. 2. Sentence. 3. To cution: But because this Method is less Capacities, and hath something humane all to these following Heads.

1. I will shew what Judgment is.
2. Who is the Judg: and why.
3. Who must be judg'd.
4. Who is the Accuser.
5. How the Citation, Constraint a will be.
6. What is the Law by which Men sh
7. What will be the Cause of the Accusation, and what must be the ju
8. What will be the Evidence.

9. What are those frivolous insufficient Excuses by which the Unrighteous may think to escape.

10. What will be the Sentence, who shall *die*, and who shall *live*, and what the Reward and Punishment is.

11. What are the Properties of the Sentence.

12. What and by whom the Execution will be. In these particular Heads we contain the whole Doctrine of this Judgment, and in this more familiar Method shall handle it.

I. For the first Judgment, as taken *largely*, comprehendeth all the forementioned Particulars; as taken more *strictly* for the Act of the Judg, it is *the Trial of a controverted Case*. In our Case note these things following.

1. God's Judgment is not intended for any Discovery to himself of what he knows not already, he knows already that all Men are, and what they have done, and what is their Due: But it is to discover to others and to Men themselves the ground of his Sentence, that so his Judgment may attain its End, for the glorifying his Grace on the Righteous, and for the convincing the Wicked of their Sin and Desert, and to shew to all the World the Righteousness of the Judg, and of his Sentence and Execution. *Rom.* 3. 4, 26. and *Rom.* 2. 2.

2. It is not a Controversy therefore undecided in the Mind of God, that is there to be decided; but only one that is undecided, as to the Knowledg and Mind of Creatures.

3. Yet is not this Judgment *a bare Declaration*, but *a Decision*, and so *a Declaration* thereupon: the Cause will be then put out of Controversy, and all farther Expectation of Decision be at an End; and with the Justified there will be no more Accusation, and with the Condemned no more Hope for ever.

II. For the second Thing, who shall be the Judg; I answer, The Judg is *God himself by Jesus Christ*.

1. Principally, God as Creator.

2. As also, God as Redeemer; the humane Nature of Jesus Christ having a derived subordinate Power. God lost not his Right to his Creature either by Man's Fall, or the Redemption by Christ, but by the latter hath a new farther Right: but it is in and by Christ that God judgeth: For as *meer Creator of innocent Man*, God judgeth none, but hath committed all Judgment to the Son, who hath procured this Right by the redeeming of fallen Man, *Joh.* 5. 22. But as the Son only doth it in the nearest Sense, so the Father as Creator doth it remotely and principally.

1. In that the Power of the Son is derived from the Father, and so standeth in Subordination to him as Fountain or Efficient.

2. In that the Judgment of the Son (as also his whole Mediatorship) is to bring Men to God their Maker as their ultimate End, and recover them to him from whom they are faln; and so as a Means to that End, the Judgment of the Son is subordinate to the Father.

From hence you may see these following Truths worthy your Consideration.

1. That all Men are God's Creatures, and none are the Workmanship of themselves or any other; or else the Creator should not judg them on that Right.

2. That Christ died for All, and is the Redeemer of the World, and a Sacrifice for All, or else he should not judg them on that Right. For he will not judg Wicked Men as he will do the Devils, as the *meer Enemies* of his Redeemed Ones, but as being themselves his Subjects in the World, and being bought by him, and therefore become his own, who ought to have glorified him that bought them, 2 *Cor.* 5. 14, 15. 2 *Pet.* 2. 1. 1 *Cor.* 6. 19, 20. 1 *John* 2. 2. *Heb.* 2. 9. 1 *Tim.* 2. 6, 7.

3. Hence it appeareth that all Men were under some Law of Grace, and did partake of some of the Re-

eemer's Mercy. Tho the Gospel came not to all, yet all had that Mercy which could come from no other Fountain but his Blood, and which should have brought them nearer to Christ than they were, (though it were not sufficient to bring them to Belief) and which should have led them to Repentance, *Romans* 2. 4. For the neglecting of which they justly perish, and not *merly* for sinning against the Law that was given Man in Innocency: Were that so, Christ would not judg them as Redeemer, and that for the Abuse or not Improvement of his Talents, as he tells us he will do, *Mat.* 25. *per totum.*

4. If God will be the Judg, then none can expect by any Shifts or indirect Means to escape at that Day. For how should it be?

1. It is not possible that any should keep out of *Sight*, or hide their Sin and the Evil of their Actions, and so delude the Judg: God will not be mocked now, nor deceived then, *Gal.* 6. 7. they grosly deceive themselves that imagine any such thing: God must be Omniscient and All-seeing, or he cannot be God. Should you hide your Cause from Men and from Devils, and be ignorant of it your selves, yet cannot you hide it from God. Never did there a Thought pass thy Heart, or a Word pass thy Mouth, which God was not acquainted with: and as he knows them, so doth he observe them. He is not as imperfect Man, taken up with other Business, so that he cannot mind *All*. As easy is it with him to observe every Thought, or Word, or Action of thine, as if he had but *that one* in the World to observe; and as easy to observe each particular Sinner, as if he had not another Creature to look after in the World. He is a Fool indeed that thinks now that God takes no notice of him, *Ezek.* 8. 12. and 9. 9. or that thinketh then to escape in the Croud: He that found out one Guest that had not on a Wedding-Garment, *Mat.* 22. 12. will then find out every unholy Soul, and give him so sad a Salutation as shall make him speechless. *Job* 11. 11. *For he*

knoweth vain Man; he seeth Wickedness also, and will he not consider it?

2. It is not possible that any should escape at that Day by any Tricks of Wit and false Reasoning in their own Defence. God knoweth a sound Answer from an unsound, and a Truth from a Lie. Righteousness may be perverted here on Earth, by out-witting the Judg; but so will it not be then. To hope any of this, is to hope that God will not be God. It is in vain then for the *unholy* Man to say he is *holy*; or for any Sinner to deny, or excuse, or extenuate his Sin; to bring forth the Counterfeit of any Grace, and plead with God any Shells of hypocritical Performances, and to think to prove a Title to Heaven by any thing short of God's Condition: all these will be vain Attempts.

3. And as impossible will it prove by Fraud or Flattery, by Perswasion or Bribery, or by any other Means, to pervert Justice by turning the Mind of God who is the Judg: Fraud and Flattery, Bribery and Importunity may do much with weak Men, but with God they will do nothing. Were he changeable and partial, he were not God.

4. If God be Judg, you may see the Cavils of Infidels are foolish, when they ask, *How long will God be in trying and judging so many Persons, and taking an Account of so many Words, and Thoughts, and Deeds? Sure it will be a long Time, and a difficult Work.* As if God were as Man that knoweth not things till he seek out their Evidence by particular Signs. Let these Fools understand, if they have any Understanding, that the infinite God can shew to every Man at once, all the Thoughts, and Words, and Actions that ever he hath been guilty of. And in the twink of an Eye, even at one view, can make all the World to see their Ways and their Deservings, causing their Consciences and Memories to present them all before them in such a sort, as shall be equivalent to a verbal Debate, *Psal.* 50. 21, 22. he will set them in Order before them.

5. If

5. If Jesus Christ be the Judg, then what a Comfort must it needs be to his Members, that he shall be Judg that loved them to the Death, and whom they loved above their Lives, and he who was their Rock of Hope and Strength, and the Desire and Delight of their Souls!

6. And if Jesus Christ must be the Judg, what Confusion will it bring to the Faces of his Enemies, and of all that set light by him in the Day of their Visitation? to see Mercy turned against them, and he that died for them now ready to condemn them, and that Blood and Grace which did aggravate their Sin, to be pleaded against them to the Increase of their Misery: How sad will this be?

7. If the God of Love, and Grace, and Truth, be Judg, then no Man need to fear any Wrong. No Subtlety of the Accuser, nor Darkness of Evidence; no Prejudice or Partiality, or whatsoever else may be imagined, can there appear to the Wrong of your Cause. Get a good Cause and fear nothing: and if your Cause be bad, nothing can deliver you.

III. For the third Point, *Who are they that must be judged?*

Answ. All the rational Creatures in this lower World. And it seems Angels also, either *all* or *some*: But because their Case is more darkly made known to us, and less concerns us, we will pass it by. Every Man that hath been made or born on Earth (except Christ, who is God and Man, and is the Judg) must be judged. If any foolish Infidels shall say, *Where shall so great a Number stand?* I answer him, That he knoweth not the things Invisible; either the Nature of Spirits and spiritual Bodies, nor what Place containeth them, or *how*; but easily he may know that he that gave them all a Being, can sustain them all, and have room for them all, and can at once disclose the Thoughts of all, as I said before.

The first in Order to be judged are the Saints, *Mat.* 25. and then with Christ they shall judg the rest of the World, 1 *Cor.* 6. 2, 3. not in an equal Authority and Commission with Christ, but as the present Approvers of his righteous Judgment. The Princes of the Earth shall stand then before Christ even as the Peasants, and the Honourable as the Base; the Rich and the Poor shall meet together, and the Lord shall judg them all, *Prov.* 22. 2. No Men shall be excused from standing at that Bar, and giving up their Account, and receiving their Doom. Learned and unlearned, young and old, godly and ungodly, all must stand there. I know some have vainly imagined that the Righteous shall not have any of their Sins mentioned, but their Graces and Duties only; but they consider not that things will not then be transacted by Words as we do now, but by clear Discoveries by the infinite Light; and that if God should not discover to them their Sins he would not discover the Riches of his Grace in the Pardon of all these Sins: even then they must be humbled in themselves that they may be glorified, and for ever cry, Not unto us Lord, but unto thy Name be the Glory.

IV. For the fourth Particular, *Who will be the Accuser?*

Answ. 1. Satan is called in Scripture the Accuser of the Brethren, *Revel.* 12. 10. and we find in *Job* 1. and other Places, that now he doth practise it even before God: and therefore we judg it probable that he will do so then. But we would determine of nothing that Scripture hath not clearly determined.

2. Conscience will be an Accuser, though especially of the Wicked, yet in some sense of the Righteous, for it will tell the Truth to all; and therefore so far as Men are faulty, it will tell them of their Faults. The Wicked it will accuse of unpardoned Sin, and of Sin unrepented of; the Godly only of Sin repented of and

pardoned. It will be a Glass wherein every Man may see the Face of his Heart and former Life, Rom. 1. 5.

3. The Judg himself will be the principal Accuser; for it is he that is wronged, and he that prosecutes the Cause, and will do Justice on the Wicked. God judgeth even the Righteous themselves to be Sinners, or else they could not be pardoned Sinners. But he judgeth the Wicked to be impenitent, unbelieving, unconverted Sinners. Remember what I said before, that it is not a verbal Accusation, but an opening of the Truth of the Cause to the view of our selves and others, that God will then perform.

Nor can any think it unworthy of God to be Mens Accuser by such a Disclosure, it being no Dishonour to the purest Light to reveal a Dunghil, or to the greatest Prince to accuse a Traitor. Nor is it unmeet that God should be both Accuser and Judg, seeing he is both absolute Lord, and perfectly Just, and so far beyond all suspicion of Injustice. His Law also doth virtually accuse, *Joh.* 5. 45. but of this by it self.

V. For the fifth Particular, *How will the Sinners be called to the Bar?*

Answ. God will not stand to send them a Citation, nor require them to make their voluntary Appearance: but willing or unwilling he will bring them in.

1. Before each Man's particular Judgment, he sendeth Death to call away his Soul, a surly Serjeant that will have no Nay: How dear soever this World may be to Men, and how loth soever they are to depart, away they must, and come before the Lord that made them; Death will not be bribed. Every Man that was set in the Vineyard in the Morning of their Lives, must be called out at Evening to receive according to what he hath done: then must the naked Soul alone appear before its Judg, and be accountable for all that was done in the Body, and be sent before till the final Judgment

to

to remain in Happineſs or Miſery, till the Body be raiſed again and joined to it.

In this Appearance of the Soul before God, it ſeemeth by Scripture, that there is ſome Miniſtry of Angels; for *Luke* 16. 22. it is ſaid that the Angels carried *Lazarus*, that is, his Soul, into *Abraham*'s Boſom. What local Motion there is, or Situation of Souls, is no fit Matter for the Enquiry of Mortals; and what it is in this that the Angels will do, we cannot clearly underſtand as yet; but moſt certain it is, that as ſoon as ever the Soul is out of the Body, it comes to its account before the God of Spirits.

2. At the end of the World the Bodies of all Men ſhall be raiſed from the Earth, and joined again to their Souls, and the Soul and Body ſhall be judged to their endleſs State; and this is the great and general Judgment where all Men ſhall at once appear. The ſame Power of God that made Men of nothing, will as eaſily then new-make them by a Reſurrection, by which he will add much more Perfection, even to the Wicked in their Naturals, which will make them capable of the greater Miſery; even they ſhall have immortal and incorruptible Bodies, which may be the Subjects of immortal Wo, 1 *Cor.* 15. 53. *John* 5. 28, 29.

Of this Reſurrection and our Appearance at Judgment, the Angels will be ſomeway the Miniſters: as they ſhall come with Chriſt to Judgment, ſo they ſhall ſound his Trumpet, 1 *Theſſ.* 4 16. and they ſhall gather the Wicked out of God's Kingdom, and they ſhall gather the Tares to burn them, *Matth.* 13. 39, 40, 41. in the End of the World the Angels ſhall come forth and ſever the Wicked from among the Juſt, and ſhall caſt them into the Furnace of Fire, *Matth.* 17. 49, 50.

VI. For the ſixth Particular, *What Law is it that Men ſhall be judged by?*

Answ. That which was given them to live by: God's Law is but *the Sign of his Will to teach us what shall be due from us and to us:* before we fell he gave us such a Law as was sutable to our Perfection; when we had sinned and turned from him, as we ceased not to be his Creatures, nor he to be our Lord, so he destroyed not his Law, nor discharged or absolved us from the Duty of our Obedience. But because we stood condemned by that Law, and could not be justified by it, having once transgressed it, he was pleased to make a *Law of Grace*, even *a new, a remedying Law*, by which we might be saved from the deserved Punishment of the Old. So we shall be tried at Judgment upon *both* these Laws, but ultimately upon the last. The first Law commanded perfect Obedience, and threatned Death to us if ever we disobeyed; the second Law finding us under the Guilt of Sin against the first, doth command us to repent and believe in Christ, and so return to God by him, and promiseth us pardon of all our Sins upon that Condition, and also if we persevere, everlasting Glory. So that in Judgment though it must be first evinced that we are Sinners, and have deserved Death according to the Law of pure Nature; yet that is not the Upshot of the Judgment. For the Enquiry will be next, whether we have accepted the Remedy, and so obeyed the Law of Grace, and performed its Condition for Pardon and Salvation, and upon this our Life or Death will depend. It is both these Laws that condemn the Wicked, but it is only the Law of Grace that justifieth the Righteous.

Obj. *But how shall Heathens be judged by the Law of Grace, that never did receive it?*

Answ. The express Gospel some of them had not, and therefore shall not directly be judged by it; but much of the Redeemer's Mercy they did enjoy, which should have led them to repent and seek out after Recovery from their Misery, and to come nearer Christ; and for the neglect and abuse of this they shall be judged.

and

be unsatisfied in this, let them remember that as God hath left the State of such more dark to us, and the Terms on which he will judg them; so doth it much more concern us to look to the Terms of our own Judgment.

Obj. *But how shall Infants be judged by the Gospel, that were uncapable of it?*

Answ. For ought I find in Scripture, they stand or fall with their Parents, and on the same Terms; but I leave each to their own Thoughts.

VII. For the seventh Head, *What will be the Cause of the Day to be enquired after? what the Accusation, and what the Defence?*

Answ. This may be gathered from what was last said. The great Cause of the Day will be to enquire and determine who shall die and who shall live, who ought to go to Heaven, and who to Hell for ever, according to the Law by which they must then be judged.

1. As there is a twofold Law by which they must be judged, so will there then be a twofold Accusation. The first will be that they were *Sinners*, and so having violated the Law of God, they deserve everlasting Death according to that Law. If no Defence could be made, this one Accusation would condemn all the World; for it is most certain that all are Sinners, and as certain that all Sin deserveth Death. The only Defence against this Accusation lieth in this Plea; confessing the Charge, we must plead that Christ hath satisfied for Sins, and upon that Consideration God hath forgiven us; and therefore being forgiven, we ought not to be punished: To prove this we must shew the Pardon under God's Hand in the Gospel. But because this par-

doning

doning Act of the Gospel doth forgive none but those that repent and believe, and so return to God, and to sincere Obedience for the time to come; therefore the next Accusation will be, that *we did not perform these Conditions of Forgiveness; and therefore being Unbelievers, Impenitent and Rebels against the Redeemer, we have no right to Pardon, but by the Sentence of the Gospel are liable to a greater Punishment for this Contempt of Christ and Grace.* This Accusation is either *true* or *false*: where it is *true*, God and Conscience, who speak the Truth, may well be said to be the Accusers: Where it is *false*, it can be only the Work of Satan the malicious Adversary, who, as we may see in *Job*'s Case, will not stick to bring a false Accusation.

If any think that the Accuser will not do so vain a Work, at least they may see that *potentially* this is the Accusation that lieth against us, and which we must be justified against. For all *Justification* implieth an *actual* or *potential Accusation.*

He that is truly accused of final Impenitency, or Unbelief, or Rebellion, hath no other Defence to make, but must needs be condemned.

He that is falsly accused of such Non-performance of the Condition of Grace, must deny the Accusation, and plead his own personal Righteousness as against that Accusation, and produce that Faith, Repentance and sincere Obedience and Perseverance, by which he fulfilled that Condition, and so is *Evangelically Righteous* in himself, and therefore hath part in the Blood of Christ, which is instead of a *Legal Righteousness* to him in all things else, as having procured him a Pardon of all his Sins, and a Right to everlasting Glory.

And thus we must then be justified by Christ's Satisfaction only against the Accusation of being *Sinners in general*, and of deserving God's Wrath for the Breach of the Law of Works; but we must be justified by our Faith, Repentance and sincere Obedience it self, against the Accusation of being *Impenitent, Unbelievers*

and

and Rebels against Christ, and having not performed the Condition of the Promise, and so having no part in Christ and his Benefits.

So that in sum you see that the Cause of the Day will be to enquire, whether being all known Sinners, we have accepted of Christ upon his Terms, and so have Right in him and his Benefits or not? whether they have forsaken this vain World for him, and loved him so faithfully, that they have manifested it, in parting with these things at his Command? And this is the meaning of *Mat.* 25. where the Enquiry is made to be, whether they have fed and visited him in his Members or not? that is, whether they have so far loved him as their Redeemer, and God by him, as that they have manifested this to his Members according to Opportunity, though it cost them the Hazard or Loss of all; seeing Danger, and Labour, and Cost are fitter to express Love by than empty Compliments and bare Professions.

Whether it be particularly enquired after, or only taken for granted that Men are *Sinners*, and have deserved Death according to the *Law of Works*, and that Christ hath satisfied by his Death, is all one as to the matter in hand, seeing God's Enquiry is but the Discovery and Conviction of us. But the last Question which must decide the Controversy will be, whether we have performed the Condition of the Gospel?

I have the rather also said all this, to shew you in what sense these Words are taken in the Text, that *every Man shall be judged according to what he hath done in the Flesh, whether it be good or bad.* Though every Man be judged *worthy* of Death for sinning, yet every Man shall not be judged *to die* for it, and no Man shall be judged *worthy* of Life *for* his good Works: It is therefore according to the Gospel, as the Rule of Judgment, that this is meant. They that have repented and believed, and returned to *true*, though *imperfect* Obedience, shall be judged to everlasting

Life,

Life, *according* to these Works; not because these Works *deserve* it, but because the *free Gift in the Gospel* through the Blood of Christ, doth make these things the *Condition* of our possessing it. They that have lived and died Impenitent, Unbelievers and Rebels against Christ, shall be judged to everlasting Punishment, *because* they have *deserved* it both by their Sin in *general* against the the Law, and by these Sins in *special* against the Gospel. This is called *the Merit of the Cause*, that is, what is a Man's *Due* according to the true meaning of the Law, though the Due may be by free Gift. And thus you see what will be the Cause of the Day, and the Matter to be enquired after and decided as to our Life or Death.

VIII. The next Point in our Method is, to shew you, *What will be the Evidence of the Cause?*

Answ. There is a fivefold Evidence among Men. 1. When the Fact is notorious. 2. The Knowledg of an unsuspected competent Judg. 3. The Parties Confession. 4. Witness. 5. Instruments and visible Effects of the Action. All these Evidences will be at hand, and any one of them sufficient for the Conviction of the guilty Person at that Day.

1. As the Sins of *all Men*, so the *Impenitency* and *Rebellion* of the *Wicked* was notorious, or at least will be then. For though some play the Hypocrites, and hide the Matter from the World and themselves, yet God shall open their Hearts and former Lives to themselves, and to the view of all the World. He shall set their Sins in Order before them, so that it shall be utterly in vain to deny or excuse them. If any Men will then think to make their Cause as good to God as they can now do to us, that are not able to see their Hearts, they will be foully mistaken. Now they can say they have as good Hearts as the best: then God will bring them out in the Light, and shew them to themselves and all the World, whether they were good or bad. Now they will face us down that they do truly

them. We cannot now make Men acquainted with their own unsanctified Hearts, nor convince them that have not true Faith, Repentance or Obedience, but God will convince them of it; they can find Shifts and false Answers to put off a *Minister* with, but *God* will not so be shifted off. Let *us* preach as plainly to them as we can, and do all that ever we are able to acquaint them with the Impenitency and Unholiness of their own Heart, and the Necessity of a new Heart and Life, yet we cannot do it, but they will believe whether we will or not, that the old Heart will serve the turn. But how easily will *God* make them know the contrary? *We* plead with them in the dark, for though we have the Candle of the Gospel in our hands when we come to shew them their Corruption, yet they shut their Eyes and are wilfully blind; but *God* will open their Eyes whether they will or not, not by *holy Illumination*, but by *forced Conviction*; and then he will plead with them as in the open Light. *See here thy own unholy Soul; canst thou now say thou didst love me above all? canst thou deny but thou didst love this World before me, and serve thy Flesh and Lusts, though I told thee if thou didst so thou shouldst die? Look upon thy own Heart now, and see whether it be an holy or an unholy Heart, a spiritual or a fleshly Heart, a heavenly or an earthly Heart. Look now upon all the Course of thy Life, and see whether thou didst live to me, or to the World and thy Flesh.* O how easily will God convince Men then of the very Sins of their Thoughts, and in their secret Closets, when they thought that no Witness could have disclosed them! Therefore it's said that the Books shall be opened, and the Dead judged out of the Books, *Rev.* 20. 12. *Dan.* 7. 10.

The second Evidence will be *the Knowledg of the Judg.* If the *Sinner* would not be *convinced*, yet it is sufficient that the *Judg* knoweth the Cause; God needeth no farther Witness, he saw thee committing Adultery in secret,

secret, Lying, Stealing, Forswearing in secret. If thou do not know thine own Heart to be unholy, 'tis enough that God knoweth it. If you have the Face to say, *Lord, when did we see thee hungry?* &c. *Mat.* 25. 44. yet God will make good the Charge against thee, and there needeth no more Testimony than his own. Can foolish Sinners think to lie hid or escape at that Day, that will now sin *wilfully before their Judg?* that know every Day that their *Judg* is *looking* on them, while they forget him, and give up themselves to the World, and yet go on even under his Eye, as if to his Face they dared him to punish them?

3. The third Evidence will be, *the Sinners Confession* God will force their own Consciences to witness against them, and their own Tongues to confess the Accusation. If they do at first excuse it, he will leave them speechless, yea and condemning themselves before they have done.

O what a difference between their Language now and then! *Now* we cannot tell them of their Sin and Misery, but they either tell us of our own Faults, or bid us look to our selves, or deny or excuse their Fault, or make light of it: but *then* their own Tongues shall confess them, and cry out of the wilful Folly that they committed, and lay a heavier Charge upon them than we can now do. *Now* if we tell them that we are afraid they are unregenerate, and lest their Hearts are not truly set upon God, they will tell us they hope to be saved with such Hearts as they have: But *then*, O how they will confess the Folly and Falseness of their own Hearts! You may see a little of their Case even in despairing Sinners on Earth, how far they are from denying or excusing their Sins. *Judas* cries out, *I have sinned in betraying innocent Blood*, Mat. 27. 4. out of their own Mouth shall they be judged. That very Tongue that now excuseth their Sin, will in their Torments be their great Accuser. For God will have it so to be.

4. The fourth Evidence will be the *Witneſs of others.* O how many thouſand Witneſſes might there be produced, were there need, to convince the guilty Soul at that Day!

1. All the Miniſters of Chriſt that ever preached to them, or warned them, will be ſufficient Witneſſes againſt them; *we muſt needs* teſtify that we preached to them the Truth of the Goſpel, and they would not believe it. We preached to them the Goodneſs of God, yet they ſet not their Hearts upon him; we ſhewed them their Sin, and they were not humbled: we told them of the danger of an unregenerate State, and they did not regard us: we acquainted them with the abſolute Neceſſity of Holineſs, but they made light of all: we let them know the Deceitfulneſs of their Hearts, and the need of a cloſe and faithful Examination, but they would not beſtow an Hour in ſuch a Work, nor ſcarce once be afraid of being miſtaken and miſcarrying. We let them know the Vanity of this World, and yet they would not forſake it, no not for Chriſt and the Hopes of Glory: we told them of the everlaſting Felicity they might attain, but they would not ſet themſelves to ſeek it.

What we ſhall think of it *then* the Lord knows, but ſurely it ſeemeth now to us a matter of very ſad Conſideration, that we muſt be brought in as Witneſſes againſt the Souls of our Neighbours and Friends in the Fleſh. Thoſe whom we now unfeignedly love, and would do any thing that we were able to do for their good, whoſe Welfare is dearer to us than all worldly Enjoyments. Alas, that we muſt be forced to teſtify to their Faces for their Condemnation! Ah Lord, with what a Heart muſt a poor Miniſter ſtudy, when he conſidereth this, that all the Words that he is ſtudying muſt be brought in for a Witneſs againſt many of his Hearers! with what an Heart muſt a Miniſter preach when he remembreth that all the Words that he is ſpeaking muſt condemn many, if not moſt of his Hearers? Do we de-

ſire

fire this ſad Fruit of our Labours? No, we may ſay with the Prophet, *Jer.* 17. 16. *I have not deſired the woful Day thou knoweſt:* No, if we deſired it, we would not do ſo much to prevent it, we would not ſtudy, and preach, and pray, and intreat Men, that if it were poſſible we might not be put on ſuch a Task. And doubtleſs it ſhould make every honeſt Miniſter ſtudy hard, and pray hard, and intreat hard, and ſtoop low to Men, and be earneſt with Men in ſeaſon and out of ſeaſon, that if it may be they may not be the Condemners of their Peoples Souls. But if Men will not hear, and there be no remedy, who can help it? Chriſt himſelf came not into the World to condemn Men, but to ſave them, and yet he will condemn thoſe that will not yield to his ſaving Work: God takes no Pleaſure in the Death of a Sinner, but rather that he repent and return and live, *Ezek.* 18. 23, 32. and yet he will rejoice over thoſe to do them hurt, and deſtroy them that will not return, *Deut.* 28. 63. And if we muſt be put on ſuch a Work, he will make us like-minded. The Holy Ghoſt tells us that the Saints ſhall judg the World, 1 *Cor.* 6. 2, 3. and if they muſt judg, they will judg as God judgeth; you cannot blame us for it, Sinners: we now warn you of it before-hand, and if you will not prevent it, blame not us but your ſelves. Alas, we are not our own Maſters! As we now ſpeak not to you in our own Names, ſo then we may not do what we liſt our ſelves, or if we might, our Wills will be as God's Will. God will make us judg you and witneſs againſt you. Can we abſolve you when the righteous God will condemn you? when God is againſt you, whoſe ſide would you have us be of? we muſt be either againſt *God* or *you*; and can you think that we ſhould be for any one againſt our Maker and Redeemer? we muſt either condemn the Sentence of Jeſus Chriſt or condemn you: and is not there more reaſon to condemn you than him? Can we have any Mercy on you, when he that made you will not ſave you, and he that formed you will ſhew you no Mercy? *Iſa.* 27. 11. yea when he that died for you will condemn you, ſhall we be more merciful than God? But alas! if we ſhould be ſo fooliſh and unjuſt, what good would it do you? If we would be Falſe-witneſſes and partial Judges, it would not ſave you; we are not juſtified if we abſolve our ſelves, 1 *Cor.* 4. 4. how unable then ſhall we be againſt God's Sentence to juſtify you? If all the World ſhould ſay you were holy and penitent, when God knows you were unholy and impenitent, it will do you no good. You pray every Day that *his Will* may be done, and it will be done: It will be done *upon* you, becauſe it was not done *by* you. What would you have *us* ſay, if God ask us, *Did you tell this Sinner of the need of Chriſt, of the Glory of the World to come, and the Vanity of this?* Should we lie and ſay we did not? What ſhould we ſay if he ask us, *Did not you tell them the Miſery of their natural State, and what would become of them if they were not made new?* Would you have us lie to God, and ſay we did not? Why if we *did not*, your Blood will be required at our hands, *Ezek.* 33. 6. and 3. 18. and would you have us bring your Blood upon our own Heads by a Lie? yea, and to do you no good, when we know that Lies will not prevail with God? No, no, Sinners; we muſt unavoidably teſtify to the Confuſion of your Faces; if God ask us, we muſt bear Witneſs againſt you and ſay, *Lord, we did what we could according to our weak Abilities to reclaim them: indeed our own Thoughts of everlaſting Things were ſo low, and our Hearts ſo dull, that we muſt confeſs we did not follow them ſo cloſe, nor ſpeak ſo earneſtly as we ſhould have done: we did not cry ſo loud, or lift up our Voice as a Trumpet to awaken them* (Iſa. 58. 1.) *we confeſs we did not ſpeak to them with ſuch melting Compaſſion, and with ſuch Streams of Tears beſeech them to regard, as a Matter of ſuch great Concernment ſhould have been ſpoken with; we did not fall on our Knees to them, and ſo earneſtly beg of them for the Lord's ſake, to have Mercy upon their own Souls as we ſhould have done. But yet we told them the Meſſage of God,* of it, Mat. 22. 5. we would fain have brought them to the Contempt of this vain World, and to set their Mind on the World to come, but we could not. Some Compassion thou knowest, Lord, we had to their Souls, many a weeping and groaning Hour we have had in secret, because they would not hear and obey, and some sad Complaints we have made over them in publick: we told them that they must shortly die and come to Judgment, and that this World would deceive them and leave them in the Dust: we told them that the time was at hand when nothing but Christ would do them good, and nothing but the Favour of God would be sufficient for their Happiness, but we could never get them to lay it to heart. Many a time did we intreat them to think soberly of this Life and the Life to come, and to compare them together with the Faith of Christians and the Reason of Men, but they would not do it: many a time did we intreat them but to take now and then an Hour in secret to consider who made them, and for what he had made them, and why they were sent into this World, and what their Business here is, and whither they are going, and how it will go with them at their latter End: but we could never get most of them to spend one Hour in serious Thoughts of these weighty Matters. Many a time did we intreat them to try whether they were Regenerate or not, whether Christ and his Spirit were in them or not, whether their Souls were brought back to God by Sanctification; but they would not try: we did beseech them to make sure Work, and not leave such a Matter as everlasting Joy or Torment to a bold and mad Adventure, but we could not prevail. We intreated them to lay all other Businesses aside a little while in the World, and to enquire by the Direction of the Word of God, what would become of them in the World to come, and judg themselves before God came to judg them, seeing they had the Law and Rule of Judgment before them; but their Minds were blinded, and their Hearts were *hardned, and the Profit, and Pleasure, and Honour of this World did either stop their Ears, or quickly steal away their Hearts, so that we could never get them to a sober Consideration, nor ever win their Hearts to God.*

This will be the Witness that many a hundred Ministers of the Gospel must give in against the Souls of their People at that Day. Alas, that ever you should cast this upon us! For the Lord's sake, Sirs, pity your poor Teachers if you pity not your selves. We had rather go 1000 Miles for you, we had rather be scorned and abused for your sakes, we had rather lay our Hands under your Feet, and beseech you on our Knees with Tears, were we able, than be put on such Work as this. It is *you* that will do it if it be done. We had rather follow you from House to House, and teach and exhort you, if you will but hear us and accept of our Exhortation. Your Souls are precious in our Eyes, for we know they were so in the Eyes of Christ, and therefore we are loth to see this Day; we were once in your Case, and therefore know what it is to be blind, and careless and carnal as you are, and therefore would fain obtain your Deliverance. But if you *will* not hear, but we *must* accuse you, and we *must* condemn you, the Lord judg between you and us. For we can witness that it was full sore against our Wills. We have been faulty indeed in doing no more for you, and not following you with restless Importunity, (the Good Lord forgive us) but yet we have not betrayed you by silence.

2. All those that fear God, that have lived among ungodly Men, will also be sufficient Witnesses against them. Alas, they must be put upon the same Work, which is very unpleasant to their Thoughts, as Ministers are! They must witness before the Lord that they did as Friends and Neighbours admonish them; that they gave them a good Example, and endeavoured to walk in Holiness before them. But alas, the most did but mock them, and call them Puritans and precise Fools, and they made more ado than needs for their

Salvation:

Salvation: They must be forced to testify, [Lord, we would fain have drawn them with us to hear the Word and to read it, and to pray in their Families, and to sanctify the holy Day, and take such happy Opportunities for their Souls; but we could not get them to it: we did in our Places what we were able to give them the Example of a godly Conversation, and they did but deride us, they were readier to mark every slip of our Lives, and to observe all our Infirmities, and catch at any Accusation that was against us, than to follow us in any Work of holy Obedience, or Care for their everlasting Peace.] The Lord knows it is a most heavy thing to consider now that poor Neighbours must be fain to come in against those they love so dearly, and by their Testimony to judg them to Perdition. O heavy Case to think of, that a Master must witness against his own Servant! Yea, a Husband against his own Wife, and a Wife against her Husband; yea, Parents against their own Children, and say, [Lord I taught them thy Word, but they would not learn; I told them what would come on it if they returned not to thee, I brought them to Sermons, and I prayed with them and for them. I frequently minded them of these everlasting Things, and of this dreadful Day which they now see. But youthful Lusts and the Temptations of the Flesh and the Devil led them away, and I could never get them throughly and soundly to lay it to their Hearts.] O you that are Parents, and Friends, and Neighbours, in the Fear of God bestir you now, that you may not be put to this at that Day of Judgment. O give them no rest, take no nay of them till you have perswaded their Hearts from this World to God, lest you be put to be their Condemners: It must be *now* that you must prevent it, or else *never*; *now* while you are with them, while you and they are in the Flesh together, which will be but a little while: Can you but now prevail with them, all will be well, and you may meet them joyfully before the Lord.

3. Another Witness that will testify against the Ungodly at that Day, will be their sinful Companions, those that drew them into Sin, or were drawn by them, or joined with them in it. O little do poor Drunkards think, when they sit merrily in an Ale-house, that one of them must bear witness against another, and condemn one another! If they thought of this, methinks it should make them have less Delight in that Company: those that now join with you in Wickedness, shall then be forced to witness, [I confess, Lord, I did hear him swear and curse, I heard him deride those that feared the Lord, and make a Jest of a holy Life: I saw him in the Ale-house when he should be hearing the Word of God, or reading, or calling upon God, and preparing for this Day: I joined with him in fleshly Delights, in abusing thy Creature and our own Bodies.] Sinners, look your Companions in the Face the next time you are with them, and remember this that I now say; that those Men shall give in Evidence against you, that now are your Associates in all your Mirth. Little thinketh the Fornicator and lustful Wanton, that their sinful Mates must then bear Witness of that which they thought the Dark had concealed, and tell their Shame before all the World. But this must be the Fruit of Sin. It's meet that they who encouraged one another in Sin, should condemn one another for it. And marvel not at it, for they shall be forced to it whether they will or no; Light will not then be hid: They may think to have some ease to their Consciences, by accusing and condemning others. When *Adam* is questioned for his Sin, he presently accuseth the Woman, *Gen.* 3. 12. when *Judas* his Conscience was awakned, he runs to the Pharisees with the Money that drew him to it, and they cast it back in his own Face, *See thou to it, what is that to us?* *Mat.* 27. 4, 5, 6. O the cold Comfort that Sinners will have at that Day, and the little Pleasure that they will find in remembring their evil Ways! *Now* when a Fornicator or a Worldling, or a

merry voluptuous Man is grown old, and cannot act all his Sin again, he takes Pleasure in remembring and telling others of his former Folly; what he once was, and what he did, and the merry Hours that he had: but *then* when Sinners are come to themselves a little more, they will remember and tell one another of these things with another Heart. O that they did but know now how these things will then affect them!

4. Another Witness that will then rise up against them, will be the very Devils that tempted them: They that did purposely draw them to Sin, that they might draw them to Torment for Sin: They can witness that you hearkned to their Temptations, when you would not hearken to God's Exhortations: They can witness that you obeyed them in working Iniquity. But because you may think the Accuser's Testimony is not to be taken, I will not stand on this. Though it is not nothing where God knoweth it to be true.

5. The very Angels of God also may be Witnesses against the Wicked; therefore are we advised in Scripture not to sin before them, *Eccl.* 5. 6. 1 *Cor.* 11. 10. 1 *Tim.* 5. 21. I charge thee before the Elect Angels, *&c.* They can testify that they would have been ministring Spirits for their good, when the Wicked rather chose to be Slaves to the Spirit of Maliciousness. The holy Angels of God do many a time stand by you when you are sinning: They see you when you see not them; they are imployed by God in some sort for your good, as well as we. And as it is the Grief of Ministers that their Labours succeed not, so may we suppose that according to their State and Nature it is theirs. For they that rejoice in Heaven at the Conversion of one Sinner, may be said to sorrow, or to lose those Joys when you refuse to be converted. These noble Spirits, these holy and glorious Attendants of Christ that shall wait upon him to Judgment, will be Witnesses against rebellious Sinners to their Confu-

ſion. Sirs, you have all in you naturally a Fear of Spirits and inviſible Powers: Fear them aright, leſt hearkning to the deceiving Spirits, and refuſing the Help of the Angels of God, and wilfully ſinning before their Faces, you ſhould cauſe them at that Day, to the Terror of your Souls, to ſtand forth as Witneſſes againſt you to your Condemnation.

6. Conſcience it ſelf will be a moſt effectual Witneſs againſt the Wicked at that Day. I before told you it will be a Diſcerner, and force them to a Confeſſion. But a farther Office it hath, even to *witneſs* againſt them. If none elſe in the World had known of their ſecret Sins, Conſcience will ſay, I was acquainted with them.

7. The Spirit of Chriſt can witneſs againſt the Ungodly that he oft moved them to repent and return, and they rejected his Motions; that he ſpoke to their Hearts in ſecret, and oft ſet in with the Miniſter, and often minded them of their Caſe, and perſwaded them to God; but they reſiſted, quenched and grieved the Spirit, *Acts* 7. 51. As the Spirit witneſſeth with the Spirits of the Righteous that they are the Children of God, *Rom.* 8. 16. ſo doth he witneſs with the Conſcience of the Wicked that they were Children of Rebellion, and therefore are juſtly Children of Wrath. This Spirit will not alway ſtrive with Men: at laſt being vexed, it will prove their Enemy, and riſe up againſt them, *Gen.* 6. 3. *Iſa.* 63. 10. If you will needs *grieve it* now, it will *grieve you* then. Were it not a Spirit of *Grace*, and were it not free Mercy that it came to offer you, the Repulſe would not have been ſo condemning, nor the Witneſs of this Spirit ſo heavy at the laſt. But it was the Spirit of Jeſus, that came with recovering Grace, which you reſiſted: And though the Wages of every Sin is Death, yet you will find that it will coſt you ſomewhat more to reject this Salvation, than to break the Creator's Law of Works. Kindneſs, *ſuch* Kindneſs will not be rejected at eaſy Rates.

Many a good Motion is now made by the Spirit ɔ the Heart of a Sinner, which he doth not so much as nce observe; and therefore doth not now remember ıem. But *then* they shall be brought to his Remembrance 'ith a witness. Many a thousand secret Motions to .epentance, to Faith, to a holy Life, will be *then* set efore the Eyes of the poor, unpardoned, trembling inner, which he had quite forgotten: And the Spi-.it of God shall testify to his Confusion. [At such :Sermon I perswaded thy Heart to repent, and thou ɔouldst not; at such a time I shewed thee the Evil of ıy Sin, and perswaded thee to have forsaken it, but ıou wouldst not; I minded thee in thy secret Thoughts, f the nearness of Judgment, and the *certainty* and *weight* f everlasting things, the need of Christ, and Faith, ıd Holiness, and of the danger of Sinning; but thou idst drown all my Motions in the Cares and Pleasures f the World. Thou harkenedst rather to the Devil ıan to me; the sensual Inclinations of thy Flesh did :revail against the strongest Arguments that I used: 'hough I shewed Reasons, undeniable Reasons, from ıy Creator, from thy Redeemer, from Nature, from race, from Heaven and from Hell; yet all would not ı much as *stop* thee, much less *turn* thee, but thou *vouldest* go on; thou *wouldest* follow thy Flesh, and now t it pay thee the Wages of thy Folly; thou *wouldest* : thy own Guide, and take thine own Course, and ɔw take what thou gettest by it.]

Poor Sinners, I beseech you in the Fear of God, the :xt time you have any such Motions from the Spirit of od, to repent, and believe, and break off your Sins, ıd the Occasions of them: consider then what a Mer-' is set before you, and how it will confound you at .e Day of Judgment, to have all these Motions brought against you, and that the Spirit of Grace it self ould be your Condemner! Alas, that Men should ıoose their own Destruction, and wilfully choose it! ıd that the Foreknowledg of these things should not ɔove them to relent.

 So

So much concerning the Witness that will be brought in against the Sinner.

5. The fifth Evidence that will be given against the Sinner will be, *The Instruments and Effects.* You know among Men, if a Man be found murdered by the high-way, and you are found standing by with a bloody Sword in your Hand; especially if there were a former Dissension between you, it will be an Evidence that will prove a *strong Presumption* that you were the Murderer; but if the Fact be certain by other Evidence, then many such things may be brought for aggravation of the Fault.

So a twofold Evidence will be brought against the Sinner from these things. One to prove him guilty of the Fact, the other to aggravate the Fault, and prove that his Sin was very great.

For the former. 1. The very Creatures which Sinners abused to sin, may be brought in against them to their Conviction and Condemnation. For though these Creatures shall be consumed with the last destroying Fire, which shall consume all the World; yet shall they have a Being in the Memory of the Sinner, (an *esse Cognitum*;) the very Wine or Ale, or other Liquor which was abused to Drunkenness, may witness against the Drunkard. The sweet Morsels by which the Glutton did please his Appetite, and all the good Creatures of God which he luxuriously devoured, may witness against him, *Luke* 16. 19, 25. He that fared deliciously every Day in this Life, was told by *Abraham* when he was dead, and his Soul in Hell, [Remember that thou in thy Life-time receivedst thy good things, and likewise *Lazarus* evil things: but now he is comforted, and thou art tormented.] Though their sweet Morsels and Cups are past and gone, yet must they be remembred at Judgment and in Hell. [Remember Son] saith *Abraham*; Yea, and *remember* he must whether he will or no; long was the Glutton in sinning, and many a pleasant bit did he taste: and so many Evidences of his Sin will lie against him, and the Sweetness will then be turned into Gall.

The very Clothing and Ornaments by which proud Persons did manifest their Pride, will be sufficient Evidence against them: as his being clothed with Purple and fine Linen, is mentioned *Luke* 16. 19.

The very Lands, and Goods, and Houses of Worldlings will be an Evidence against them: Their Gold and Silver, which the Covetous do now prefer before the everlasting Riches with Christ, will be an Evidence against them: *James* 5. 1, 2, 3, 4. *Go to now, ye rich Men, weep and howl for your Miseries that shall come upon you. Your Riches are corrupted, and your Garments Moth-eaten; your Gold and your Silver is cankered, and the Rust of them shall be a* Witness *against you, and shall eat your Flesh as it were Fire; ye have heaped Treasure together for the last Days. Behold, the Hire of the Labourers, which have reaped down your Fields, which is of you kept back by Fraud, crieth; and the Cries of them which have reaped, are entred into the Ears of the Lord of Sabbath. Ye have lived in Pleasure on the Earth, and been wanton; ye have nourished your Hearts as in a Day of Slaughter.* O that Worldlings would well consider this one Text; and therein observe whether a Life of Earthly Pleasure and fulness of worldly Glory and Gallantry, be as desirable as they imagine, and to what Time and Purpose they now lay up their Treasures; and how they must hear of these things hereafter; and what effect the review of their jovial Days will have upon their miserable condemned Souls.

2. The very Circumstances of Time, Place, and the like, may evidence against his Condemnation. The Drunkard shall remember in such an Ale-house, I was so oft drunk, and in such a Tavern I wasted my time. The Adulterer and Fornicator shall remember the very Time, the Place, the Room, the Bed, where they committed Wickedness. The Thief and Deceiver will remember the Time, Place, and the Persons they wrong-

ed, and the things which they robbed or deceived them of. The Worldling will remember the Business which he preferred before the Service of God; the worldly Matters which had more of his Heart than his Maker and Redeemer had; the Work which he was doing when he should have been praying or reading, or Catechising his Family, or thinking soberly of his latter End. A thousand of these will then come into his Mind, and be as so many Evidences against him to his Condemnation.

3. The very Effects also of Mens Sins will be an Evidence against them. The Wife and Children of a Drunkard are impoverished by his Sin; his Family and the Neighbourhood is disquieted by him. These will be so many Evidences against him. So will the Abuse of his own Reason, the enticing of others to the same Sin, and hardning them by his Example.

One covetous unmerciful Landlord doth keep an hundred, or many hundred Persons or Families in so great Necessities, and Care and Labour, that they are tempted by it to overpass the Service of God, as having scarce time for it, or any Room for it in their troubled Thoughts; all these miserable Families and Persons, and all the Souls that are undone by this Temptation, will be so many Evidences against such Oppressors.

Yea, the Poor whom they have neglected to relieve when they might; the Sick whom they have neglected to visit when they might, will all witness then against the Unmerciful, *Mat.* 25.

The many ignorant, worldly, careless Sinners, that have perished under an idle and unfaithful Minister, will be so many Witnesses against him to his Condemnation! They may then cry out against him to his Face, [I was ignorant, Lord, and he never did so much as teach me, catechise me, nor tell me of these things; I was careless, and minded the World, and he let me go on quietly, and was as careless as I, had never plainly and faithfully warned me, to waken me from my Security.] And so

›d will be required at his hands, though
so shall perish in their Sins, *Ezek.* 33. 7, 8.
these Evidences will convince Men of Sin,
nany more which will convince them of the
neir Sin. And these are so many, that it
uch lengthen my Discourse to stand on
I shall briefly touch.

ry Mercy of God in *creating* Men, in giv-
nuing their *Being* to them, will be an Evi-
ıe Aggravation of their Sin against him.
'ou abuse him by whom it is that you are
ou speak to his Dishonour that giveth you
' will you live to his Dishonour who giveth
'es? will you wrong him by his own Crea-
neglect him without whom you cannot

Redemption of Men by the Lord Jesus
be an Evidence to the exceeding Aggrava-
r Sins. You sinned against the Lord that
2 *Pet.* 2. 1. When the Feast was pre-
ıll things were ready, you made light of it,
xcuses and would not come, *Mat.* 22. 4, 5,
17, 18. Must Christ redeem you by so
from Sin and Misery, and yet will you
Servants of Sin, and prefer your Slavery
Freedom, and choose to be Satan's Drud-
han to be the Servants of God? The Sor-
ferings that Christ underwent for you, will
the Increase of your own Sorrows. As a
deemer it is that he will condemn you.
ou would be glad that it were but true
hat Christ never died for you, that you
: condemned for refusing a Redeemer, and
st him that shed his Blood for you. How
his Wounds then wound your Consciences!
n remember that to this end he both died.

all, that they which live, ſhould not henceforth live to themſelves, but to him that died for them and roſe again; *Rom*. 14. 9. 2 *Cor*. 5. 14, 15. *Mat*. 28. 18, 19, 20. 1 *Pet*. 1. 17, 18. You will then underſtand that you were not your own, but were bought with a Price; and therefore ſhould have glorified him that bought you with your Bodies and Spirits, becauſe they were his, 1 *Cor*. 6. 19, 20. This one Aggravation of your Sin will make you doubly and remedileſly miſerable, that you trod under foot the Son of God, and counted the Blood of the Covenant, wherewith you were ſanctified, an unholy thing, *Heb*. 10. 26, 27, 28, 29. and crucified to your ſelves the Son of God afreſh, and put him to open Shame, *Heb*. 6. 5, 6.

3. Moreover, all the perſonal Mercies which they received, will be ſo many Evidences for the Condemnation of the Ungodly. The very Earth that bore them, and yielded them its Fruits, while they themſelves are unfruitful to God. The Air which they breathed in, the Food which nouriſh'd them, the Clothes which cover'd them, the Houſes which they dwelt in, the Beaſts that laboured for them, and all the Creatures that died for their Uſe: All theſe may riſe up againſt them to their Condemnation. And the Judg may thus expoſtulate with them, [Did all theſe Mercies deſerve no more Thanks? Should you not have ſerved him that ſo liberally maintained you? God thought not all theſe too good for you, and did you think your Hearts and Services too good for him? He ſerved yours with the weary Labours of your fellow-Creatures; and ſhould you have grudged to bear his eaſy Yoak? They were your Slaves and Drudges, and you refuſed to be his free Servants and his Sons: They ſuffered Death to feed your Bodies, and you would not ſuffer the ſhort Forbearance of a little forbidden fleſhly Pleaſure, for the ſake of him that made you and redeemed you.]

O how many thousand Mercies of God will then be reviewed by those that neglected them, to the Horror of their Souls, when they shall be upbraided by the Judg with their base Requital! All the Deliverances from Sickness and from Danger; all the Honours, and Privileges, and other Commodities which so much contented them, will then be God's Evidences to shame them and confound them. On this Supposition doth the Apostle reprove such, Rom. 2. 4, 5, 6. *Despisest thou the Riches of his Goodness, and Forbearance, and Long-suffering, not knowing that the Goodness of God leadeth thee to Repentance? But after thy hardness and impenitent Heart, treasurest up unto thy self Wrath against the Day of Wrath, and Revelation of the righteous Judgment of God, who will render to every Man according to his Deeds.*

4. Moreover, all the Means which God used for the Recovery of Sinners in the Day of their Visitation, will rise up against impenitent Souls in Judgment, to their Condemnation. You can hear Sermons carelesly and sleepily now: but O that you would consider how the Review of them will then awake you! You now make light of the Warnings of God and Man, and of all the wholesom Advice that is given you, but God will not then make light of your Contempt. O what cutting Questions will they b[illegible] Hearts of the Ungodly, when all the means tha[illegible]used for their Good, are brought to their Re[illegible]rance on one side, and the Temptations that drew them to Sin on the other Side, and the Lord shall plead his Cause with their Consciences, and say, [Was I so hard a Master, or was my Work so unreasonable, or was my Wages so contemptible that no Perswasions could draw you into my Service? Was Satan so good a Master, or was his Work so honest and profitable, or was his Wages so desirable, that you would be so easily perswaded to do as he would have you? Was there more perswading Reason in his Allurements and Deceits, than in all my holy Words, and all the powerful Sermons that you heard, or all the

faithful

faithful Admonitions you received; or all the good Examples of the Righteous, or in all the Works of God which you beheld? Was not a Reason fetch'd from the Love of God, from the Evil of Sin, the Blood of Christ, the Judgment to come, the Glory promised, the Torments threatned, as forcible with you, and as good in your Eyes to draw you to Holiness, as a Reason from a little fleshly Delight or worldly Gain, to draw you to be unholy?]

In the Name of God, Sinners, I intreat you to bethink your selves in time, how you will sufficiently answer such Questions as these. You should have seen God in every Creature that you beheld, and have read your Duty in all his Works; what can you look upon above you, or below you, or round about you, which might not have shewed you so much of the Wisdom, and Goodness, and Greatness of your Maker, as should have convinced you that it was your Duty to be devoted to his Will? and yet you have his written Word that speaks plainer than all these; and will you despise them all? will you not see so great a Light? will you not hear so loud and constant Calls? shall God and his Ministers speak in vain? And can you think that you shall not hear of this again, and pay for it one Day? you have the Bible and other good Books by you; why do you not read them? You have Ministers at hand; why do you not go to them, and earnestly ask them, *Sirs, What must I do to be saved?* and intreat them to teach you the Way to Life: You have some Neighbours that fear God; why do you not go to them, and take their good Advice, and imitate them in the Fear of God, and in a holy Diligence for your Souls? Now is the time for you to bestir your selves; Life and Death are before you. You have Gales of Grace to further your Voyage: There are more for you than against you. God will help you: his Spirit will help you: his Ministers will help you: every good Christian will help you: the Angels themselves will help you, if you will resolvedly set your selves to the Work; and yet will you not stir? Patience is waiting on you: Mercies are enticing you: Scourges are driving you: Judgment stayeth for you: The Lights of God stand burning by you to direct you: And yet will you not stir, but lie in Darkness? And do you think you shall not hear of this? Do you think this will not one Day cost you dear?

IX. The ninth part of our Work is to shew you, *What are those frivolous Excuses by which the Unrighteous may then indeavour their Defence?*

Having already shewed you what the Defence must be, that must be sufficient to our Justification;

If any first demand, Whether the Evidence of their Sin will not so overwhelm the Sinner, that he will be speechless and past excuse? I answer, Before God hath done with him, he will be so; but it seems at first his dark Understanding, and partial corrupted Conscience will set him upon a vain Defence. For *Mat.* 7. 22, 23. Christ telleth us, that [Many will say to me in that Day, Lord, Lord, have we not prophesied in thy Name, and in thy Name have cast out Devils, and in thy Name have done many wonderful Works? And then will I profess to them, I never knew you, Depart from me ye Workers of Iniquity.] And in *Mat.* 25. 11. the foolish Virgins cry, [Lord, Lord, open to us.] And *ver.* 44. [Then shall they also answer him, saying, Lord, when saw we thee an hungred, or thirst, or a Stranger, or Naked, or Sick, or in Prison, and did not minister unto thee?] And *vers.* 24, 25. they fear not to cast some of the Causes of their neglect on God himself, [Then he which had received the one Talent came and said, Lord, I knew thou art an hard Man, reaping where thou hast not sown, and gathering where thou hast not strawed; and I was afraid, and went and hid thy Talent in the Earth; lo, there thou hast that is thine.]

It is clear then, that Excuses they will be ready to make, and their full Conviction will be in order after these Excuses, (at least as in their Minds, if not in Words) but what the particular Excuses will be, we may partly know by these Scriptures which recite them, and partly by hearing what the Ungodly do now say for themselves. And because it is for their present Benefit that I now make mention of them, that they may see the Vanity of all such Excuses, I will mention them as I now meet with them in the Mouths of Sinners in our ordinary Discourse: and these Excuses are of several sorts; some by which they would justify their Estate; some Excuses of particular Actions; and that either in whole, or in part; some by which they would put by the Penalty, though they confess the Sin; some by which they lay the blame on other Men; and in some they would cast it upon God himself. I must touch but some of them very briefly.

The first Excuse. *I am not guilty of these things which I am accused of. I did love God above all, and my Neighbour as my self. I did use the World but for Necessity, but God had my Heart.*

Answ. The All-seeing Judg doth know the contrary, and he will make thy Conscience know it: Look back, Man, upon thy Heart and Life: How seldom and how neglectfully didst thou think of God? how coldly didst thou worship him, or make any mention of him? how carelesly didst thou serve him, and think much of all that thou didst therein? Thou rather thoughtest that his Service was making more ado than needs, and didst grudg at those that were more diligent than thy self; but for the World, how heartily and how constantly didst thou seek and serve it? and yet wouldst thou now perswade the Judg that thou didst love God above all? He will shew thee thy naked Heart, and the Course of thy former Life, which shall convince thee of the contrary.

The

The Second Excuse. *I lived not in any gross Sin, but only in small Infirmities; I was no Murderer, or Adulterer, or Fornicator, or Thief, nor did I deceive or wrong any, or take any thing by violence.*

Answ. Was it not a gross Sin to love the World above God, and to neglect Christ that died for thee, and never to do him one Hour's hearty Service, but meerly to seek thy carnal self, and to live to thy Flesh? God will open thine Eyes then, and shew thee a thousand gross Sins, which thou now forgettest or makest light of; and it is not only gross Sin, but all Sin, great or small, that deserveth the Wrath of God, and will certainly bring thee under it for ever, if thou have not part in Christ to relieve thee. Wo to the Man that ever he was born that must answer in his own Name for his smallest Offences!

The third Excuse. *I did it ignorantly; I knew not that there was so much required to my Salvation. I thought less ado might have served the turn: and that if I look'd to my Body, God would take care of my Soul; and that it was better to trust him what would become of me hereafter, than to trouble my Mind so much about it. Had I known better, I would have done better.*

Answ. If you knew not better, who was it long of but your self? Did God hide these things from you? Did he not tell them you in his Word as plainly as the Tongue of Man can speak, That except you were regenerate and born again, you should not enter into the Kingdom of God? *John* 3. 3, 5. That without Holiness none should see God, *Heb.* 12. 14. That you must *strive* to enter in at the strait Gate; for many shall *seek* to enter, and shall not be able, *Luke* 13. 24. That if you lived after the Flesh, you should die: and if by the Spirit you mortified the Deeds of the Body, you should live, *Rom.* 8. 13. That if any Man have not the Spirit of Christ, the same is none of his, *Rom.* 8. 9. And to be carnally minded is Death; but to be spiritually minded is Life and Peace, *Rom.* 8. 9.

That

ſteal, *Mat.* 6. 19, 20. That you muſt ſeek firſt the Kingdom of God and the Righteouſneſs thereof, *Mat.* 6. 23. and not labour for the Food that periſheth, but for the Food that endureth to everlaſting Life, which Chriſt would have given you, *John* 6. 27. That if you be riſen with Chriſt, you muſt ſeek thoſe things which are above, where Chriſt ſitteth at the right hand of God, and not the things that are on Earth, *Col.* 3. 1, 2, 3. Yea your very Converſation ſhould be in Heaven, *Phil.* 3. 19, 20, 21.

What ſay you? Did not God tell you all this and much more; and plainly tell it you? Turn to your Bibles and ſee the Words, and let them witneſs againſt you.

2. And could you think with any Reaſon, that your Souls being ſo much more precious than your Bodies, you ſhould yet do ſo much more for your Bodies than your Souls? could you think all the Labour of your Lives little enough for a frail Body that muſt lie ſhortly in the Dirt; and that your Immortal Souls ſhould be no more regarded? Could you think with any Reaſon, that your Souls ſhould do ſo much for a Life of a few Years continuance, and do no more for a Life that ſhall have no end?

3. And whereas you talk of *truſting God with your Souls*, you did not truſt him: You did but on that Pretence, careleſly diſregard them. If you truſt God, ſhew any Word of Promiſe that ever he gave you to truſt upon, that ever an impenitent, carnal, careleſs Perſon ſhall be ſaved: No; he hath told you enough to the contrary. And could you think that it was the Will of God that you ſhould mind your Bodies more than your Souls, and this Life more than that to come?

What

Why, he hath bid you strive, and run, and fight, and labour, and care, and seek, and use Violence, and all Diligence for the safety of your Souls, and for the Life to come: But where hath he bid you do so for your Bodies? No, he knew that you were prone to do too much for them; and therefore he hath bid you [Care not, and labour not] that is, Do it as if you did it not: and let your Care and Labour for earthly Things be none in comparison of that for heavenly Things. You know God can as well maintain your Lives without your Care and Labour, as save your Souls without it: And yet you see he will not, he doth not: You must plough, and sow, and reap, and thresh, for all God's Love and Care of you, and not say, I will let all alone and trust God. And must you not much more use diligence in much greater Things? If you will trust God, you must trust him in his own Way, and in the use of his own Means.

The fourth Excuse. *I was never brought up to Learning, I cannot so much as read: nor did my Parents ever teach me any of these things, but only set me about my worldly Business, and provide Food and Raiment for me: but never once told me that I had a Soul to save or lose, and an everlasting Life to provide and prepare for, and therefore I could not come to the Knowledg of them.*

Answ. The greater is their Sin who thus neglected you. But this is no sufficient Excuse for you. Heaven is not prepared for the Learned only; nor will Christ ask you at Judgment whether you are good Scholars or not, no nor so much as whether you could write or read. But consider well, Was not God's Word so plainly written, that the Unlearned might understand it? Did he not put it into the most familiar Stile, though he knew it would be offensive to the proud Scholars of the World, of purpose that he might fit it to the Capacities of the Ignorant? And if you could not read, yet tell me, could not you have learned to read at 20 or 30 Years of Age, if you had been

been but willing to bestow now and then an Hour to that end? Or at least, did you not live near some that could read? and could you not have procured them to read to you, or to help you? and did you not hear these things read to you in the Congregation by the Minister, or might have done if you would? and if your Parents did neglect you in your Youth, yet when you came to a fuller use of Reason, and heard of the Matters of Salvation from God's Word, did it not concern you to have looked to your selves, and to have redeemed that time which you lost in your Youth, by doubling your Diligence when you came to riper Years? The Apostles gathered Churches among Heathens that never heard of Christ before; and converted many thousand Souls that were never once told of a Saviour, or the Way to Salvation, till they had past a great part of their Lives. If you loitered till the latter part of the Day, it behoved you then to have bestirred your selves the more; and not to say, Through the Fault of my Parents, I lost the beginning of my Life, and therefore I will lose all; they taught me not then, and therefore I will not learn now: Have you not seen some of your Neighbours who were as ill educated as your selves, attain to much Knowledg afterwards by their Industry? and why might not you have done so, if you had been as industrious as they? May not God and Conscience witness, that it was because you cared not for Knowledg, and would not be at pains to get it, that you knew no more? Speak truth, Man, in the Presence of thy Judg; was thy Heart and Mind set upon it? Didst thou pray daily for it to God? Didst thou use all the means thou couldst to get it? Didst thou attend diligently on the Word in publick, and think of what thou heardst when thou camest home? Didst thou go to the Minister, or to others that could teach thee, and intreat them to tell thee the Way to Salvation? Or didst thou not rather carelesly neglect these Matters, and hear a Sermon as a common tale, even when the Minister was speaking of Heaven or of Hell? It was not then thine unavoidable Ignorance, but thy Negligence.

Yea further, answer as in the Presence of God; Didst thou obey so far as thou *didst know?* Or didst thou not rather sin against that Knowledg which thou hadst? Thou knewest that the Soul was better than the Body, and everlasting Life more to be regarded than this transitory Life; but didst thou regard it accordingly? Thou sure knewest that God was better than the World, and Heaven than Earth: at least thou wast told of it, but didst thou accordingly value him, and love him more? Thou knewest sure that there was no Salvation without Faith, and Repentance, and newness of Life, and yet they were neglected. In a word, many a thousand Sins which were committed, and Duties that were omitted against thy own Knowledg and Conscience, will marr this Excuse.

The fifth Excuse. *I lived not under a powerful Minister to tell me of these things; but where there was no preaching at all.*

Answ. And might you not have gone where a powerful Minister was, with a little pains? Yea, did not the very plain Word that you heard read, tell you of these things? and might you not have had a Bible your selves, and found them there?

The sixth Excuse. *I was a Servant, and had no time from my Labour to mind these matters; I lived with an hard Master that required all his own Work of me, but would allow me no time for the Service of God.* Or else, *I was a poor Man, and had a great Charge to look after, and with my hard Labour had much ado to live, so that I had no time for heavenly things.*

Answ. 1. Who should be first served, God or Man? What should be first sought after, Heaven or Earth? Did not Christ tell thee, *One thing is necessary? Luke* 10. 41, 42. Was it not as needful to see that you escape Damnation, and get safe to Heaven when this Life is ended, as to see that you had Food and Raiment for your selves and yours?

2. Did you spend no time in Recreation, nor Idleness, nor vain talking? why might not that at least have been spent about heavenly things?

3. Could you have taken no time from your rest, or eating, or at other Intermissions? Man's Body will not endure so great Labours as have no Intermission. And why then might not Godliness have been your Ease and Recreation?

4. Or might you not have minded these things even when you were about your Labour, if you had but a Heart to them?

5. At least you might have spent the Lord's own Day in hearing, reading and pondering of these Matters, when you were forced to forbear your worldly Labours, even by the wholesom Law of the Land. These therefore are all but vain Excuses; and God will shortly make thee speak out and plainly confess, it was not so much for want of Time or Helps, or warning, as for want of a Heart to use them well. I should have found some time, though it had been when I should have slept, if my Heart had been but set upon it.

The seventh Excuse. *Little did I think to have seen this Day: I did not believe that ever God would be so severe. I thought his Threatnings had been but to keep Men in awe; and I suspected either that the Scripture was not his Word, or else I thought he would be better than his Word. I thought all that I heard of another Life had been uncertain; and therefore was loth to let go a Certainty for an Uncertainty, and lose my present Pleasures which I had in hand for the Hopes of that which I never did see.*

Answ. He that will not know his Misery by believing to prevent it, shall know it by feeling to endure it. You were told and told again what your Unbelief would bring you to. Did God's Word make Heaven and Earth? doth it support them, and secure them? and

is

is not his Word sufficient Security for you to have trusted your Souls upon? did you know where was any better Security to be had? and where was any surer Ground for your Confidence? And did you think so basely and blasphemously of God, that he would falsify his Word, lest such as you should suffer? and that he was fain to rule the World by a Lie? Did God make the World so easily? and can he not govern it by true and righteous Means? what need God to say that which he will not do, to awe Sinners? can he not awe them by Truth? is it not just that those should eternally perish, that will entertain such desperate Thoughts of God, and then by such wicked Imaginations encourage themselves in Sin against him?

And for the Truth of Scripture, God did not bid you believe it without Evidence. He stamped on it the Image of his own Purity and Perfection, that you might know it by that Image and Superscription, if you had Eyes to see them: He sealed it by uncontrouled Multitudes of Miracles: He delivered it down to your hands by infallible Witnesses, so that he left you no room for rational Doubting.

And you knew that the Matters of this World were not only uncertain, but certainly vain and transitory, and would shortly come to nothing, and leave you in distress. If it had then been uncertain whether there were a Glory and Misery hereafter, (as it was not) should not Reason have taught you to prefer the least Probabilities of an everlasting unspeakable Happiness, before that which is certainly perishing and vain? These vain Excuses will but condemn you.

The eighth Excuse. *I was so enticed and perswaded by Sinners to do as they did, that I could not deny them: they would never let me rest.*

Answ. And were you not as earnestly perswaded by God to forsake Sin and serve him, and yet that would not prevail with you? You could not deny the Devils and Fools, but you could deny God and all his Messengers. Were not Ministers as earnest with you every Week to repent and amend? What did Men entice you with? with a little deluding fleshly Pleasure for a few Days? And what did God entice you with? with the Promise of endless unconceivable Felicity! And if this were a smaller Matter in your Eyes than the other, then you have had your choice; be content with it, and thank your selves. In your Life-time you had the good things which you chose, and preferred before Heaven, and therefore cannot expect to have Heaven besides.

The ninth Excuse. *I lived among ungodly Persons, that derided all that feared God; so that if I had not done as they did, but had made any more ado to be saved, I should have been the very Scorn of the Place where I lived.*

Answ. And was not Heaven worth the [illegible]ing of a Scorn? Is not he worthy to go without it that thinks so basely of it? Did not Christ tell you that if you were ashamed of him before Men, he would be ashamed of you before his Father and the Angels of Heaven? *Mark* 8. 38. He suffered more than Scorns for you: and could not you suffer a Scorn for him and your selves? seeing you chose rather to endure everlasting Torment, than a little derision from ignorant Men, take that which you made choice of. And seeing so small a Matter would drive you from Heaven, and part God and you, as a Mock, as the Wind of a Man's Mouth, no wonder if you be commanded to Depart from him into everlasting Fire.

The tenth Excuse. *I had ungodly Persons to my Parents, or Masters, or Landlord, or Governours, who threatned to* dreadful than God? Is Death more terrible than Hell? Did not Christ bid you *fear not them that can kill the Body, and after that can do no more; but fear him that is able to destroy both Body and Soul in Hell-fire; yea I say unto you, fear him?* Mat. 10. 28. Luke 12. 4, 5. and Isa. 51. 7. *Fear ye not the Reproach of Men, neither be afraid of their Revilings. For the Moth shall eat them up like a Garment, and the Worm shall eat them like Wool: but my Righteousness shall be for ever, and my Salvation from Generation to Generation.* Seeing therefore you have chosen rather to suffer from God for ever for your Sin, than to suffer small Matters for well-doing for a Moment, you must ever bear your own Choice. Christ told you before-hand, that if you could not forsake all the World and your own Lives for him, you could not be his Disciples, *Mat.* 10. 37, 38, 39. And seeing you thought his Terms too hard, and would needs seek you out a better Service, even take what you have chosen and found.

The eleventh Excuse. *I saw so many follow their Pleasure and their worldly Business, and never look after these higher things, and so few go the other way, that I thought sure God would not damn so great a Part of the World, and therefore I ventured to do as the most did.*

Answ. God will make good his Word upon many or few. Did you doubt of his Will, or of his Power? For his Will he hath told it you in his Word. For his Power he is as able to punish many as one Man. What is all the World to him, but as the Drop of a Bucket, as the Dust of the Ballance? He told you before-hand that the Gate was strait, and the Way to Heaven was narrow, and few did find it; and the Gate to Destruction was wide, and the Way was broad, and many did enter in at it, *Mat.* 7. 13, 14. And if you would not believe him, you must bear what your Unbelief hath brought you to. What if you had twenty Children, or Servants, or Friends, and the greater part of them should prove false to you and seek your Destruction, or prove disobedient, and turn to your Enemy? would you think it a good Excuse if the rest should do the like because of their Example? will you therefore wrong God because you see others wrong him? would you spit in the Face of your own Father if you saw others do so? God warned you, that you should not follow a Multitude to do Evil, *Exod.* 23. 2. And if yet you will *do* as most *do*, you must even *speed* as most *speed*. You should not so much consider who they be, as what they do, and whither they go, and who they forsake, and what they lose, and what strength is in the Reasons that move them to do this. And then you would find, it is *God* they forsake, it is *Sin* they choose; it is *Heaven* they lose, it is *Hell* they run into: and it is no true Reason, but Satan's Delusion and sensual Inclination that lead them to it. And should Men be imitated, be they many, or be they few, in such a Course as this?

The twelfth Excuse. *I saw so many Faults in those that were accounted Godly, and saw so much Division among them, that I thought they were as bad as others; and among so many Opinions, I knew not what Religion to be of.*

Answ. 1. A Spot is soonest seen in the fairest Cloth: And the malicious World useth to make such far worse than they are.

2. But suppose all were true that Malice saith of some, you could not say the like by others.

3. Or if you could, yet it was God's Law, and not Mens Faults that was made the Rule for you to live by: Will it excuse you that others are bad?

4. And from their diverse Opinions, you should have taken counsel at God's Word, which was right: Did you first search the Scripture impartially, as willing to know the Truth, that you might obey it? and did you pray daily that God would lead you into the Truth? and did you obey as much as you knew? Did you join with the Godly so far as they are all agreed? they are all agreed in the Fundamental Articles of Christianity,

ıgs absolutely necessary to a holy Life, ›n : that all known Sin is to be forsaken, Duty to be done. Why did you not ee with them? Alas, the Imperfections and the false Accusations of the mali-vill prove but a poor Cover for your wil-, and Christ will convince you of the : Excuses.

nth Excuse. *The Scriptures were so dark : understand them. And I saw the wisest ch in the Exposition of them, that I thought r me to trouble my self about them. If God us live according to the Scriptures, he would n them plainly, that Men might understand*

t is all plainly written according to the Subject: But a prejudiced, disaffected, ıught, disused Soul cannot at first under-ıest Teaching. The plainest Greek or nar that can be written, will be utterly n that is but newly entred the English fter many Years time that he spends in d you study hard, and pray for God's enquire of others, and wait patiently in , that you might come to farther Know-s? and were you *willing* to know even ıat called you out to self-denial, and that ın the hardest Flesh-displeasing Duties? thus, you would have admired the Light ripture, and now have rejoiced that ever and not have quarrelled at its seeming is Word might have made you *wise* to Sal-ıth done others, *Act.* 20. 32. 2 *Tim.* 3. *his Law of the Lord is perfect, converting stimony of the Lord is sure, making wise the tatutes of the Lord are right, rejoicing the nandment of the Lord is pure, enlightning the* 7, 8.

2. So much as is of Neceſſity to Salvation, is as plain as you could deſire. Yet, if you be judged by theſe, you will be condemned: For you did not obey that which was moſt plain. What Darkneſs is in ſuch Words as theſe, *Except ye repent, ye ſhall all periſh*, Luke 13. 3, 5. *Love not the World, nor the things in the World: if any Man love the World, the Love of the Father is not in him*, 1 John 2. 15. *He that will come after me, let him deny himſelf?* &c. Mat. 16. 24.

3. If there had been nothing that ſeemed difficult to you, would you not have deſpiſed its ſimplicity, and have thought your ſelves wiſe enough at the firſt Reading, and needed no more?

The fourteenth Excuſe. *There were ſo many ſeeming Contradictions in the Scripture, and ſo many ſtrange improbable things, that I could not believe it.*

Anſw. The Contradictions were in your fancy, that did not underſtand the Word which you read. Muſt the raw unexperienced Learner deſpiſe his Book or Teacher, as oft as in his Ignorance he thinks he meets with Contradictions? Did you think God was no wiſer than you, and underſtood not himſelf, becauſe you underſtood him not? Nor could reconcile his own Words, becauſe you could not reconcile them? You would needs be a Judg of the Law, inſtead of obeying it, and ſpeak evil of it rather than do it, *Jam.* 4. 11.

2. And thoſe things which you called improbable in the Word, were the Wonders of God, of purpoſe to confirm it. If it had not been confirmed by Wonders, you would have thought it unproved; and yet now it is ſo confirmed, you will not believe the Doctrine, becauſe the Witneſs ſeems incredible. And that is, becauſe they are Matters above the Power of Man: as if they were therefore above the Power of God! You ſhall at laſt have your Eyes ſo far opened, as to ſee thoſe ſeeming Contradictions reconciled, and the certainty of thoſe things which you accounted improbable: that you may be forced to confeſs the Folly of you

your Arrogancy and Unbelief: and then God will judg you in Righteousness, who presumed unrighteously to judg him and his Word.

The fifteenth Excuse. *It seemed so unlikely a thing to me, that the merciful God should damn most of the World to everlasting Fire, that I could not believe it.*

Answ. 1. And did it not seem as unlikely to you, that his Word should be false?

2. Should it not have seemed as unlikely that the Governour of the World should be unjust, and suffer his Law to be unexecuted, and the worst to speed as well as the best, and to suffer vile sinful Dust to despise his Mercy, and abuse his Patience, and turn all his Creatures against him without due Punishment?

3. Did you not feel Pain and Misery begin in this Life?

4. You saw Toads and Serpents which had never sinned: And you would rather live in any tolerable Suffering than be a Toad. And is it not Reason that it should go worse with contemptuous Sinners, than with those Creatures that never sinned?

5. Could you expect that those should come to Heaven, that would not believe there was such a State, but refused it, and preferred the World before it? And to be out of Heaven, is to be out of all Happiness: and he that is so out of all Happiness, and knows that he lost it by his own Folly, must needs torment himself with such Considerations, were there no other Torments. And as Man is capable of greater Felicity than Brutes, so must he needs be capable of more Misery.

The sixteenth Excuse. *The things which God promised in Heaven, and threatned in Hell, were all out of my Sight: and therefore I could not heartily believe them. Had I but once seen them, or spoke with one that had seen them, I should have been satisfied, and have contemned the things of the World.*

Answ. Will you not believe till you see or feel? Was not God's Word sufficient Evidence? would you have believed one from the dead that had told you he had seen such things? and would you not believe *Stephen* that saw them? *Act.* 7. 56. Or *Paul* that heard and saw them? 2 *Cor.* 12. 3, 4. Nor Christ that came purposely from Heaven to reveal them? why Flesh and Blood cannot see them. You see not God: will you not therefore believe that there is a God? Indeed, whatever you imagine, if you would not believe *Moses* and the Prophets, Christ and his Apostles, neither would you have believed though one had risen from the dead: For God's Word is more credible than a dead Man's: and Christ did rise from the dead to attest it. Blessed are they that have not seen, and yet believed. *Noah* saw no Rain when he was preparing the Ark: but because he *believed*, he made ready and escaped, *Heb.* 11. 7. when the World that would not *believe* did perish. But seeing God's Word was of no more weight with you, and no Knowledg would serve your turn but by *seeing* and *feeling*; you shall *see* and *feel* everlastingly to your Sorrow.

The seventeenth Excuse. *It was so strict a Law that God would have ruled me by, and the Way to Heaven was so strait and difficult, that I could not endure it. I was not able to deny my Flesh, and live such a Life.*

Answ. 1. You were not *able*, because you were not *willing*. What was there but your own wicked Hearts that should make such a Life seem grievous to you? Every thing is hard and grievous to him who loaths it, and whose Heart is against it. The chief thing that God called you to, was to *love* him, and make him your *Delight*: and are Love and Delight such grievous things? It was not grievous to you to love your Meat, or Drink, or Money: It was no hard matter to you to love a Friend that loved you; no nor to love your Sin, which was your Enemy: and what should make it seem hard to love God, but a wicked Heart? Is not he

better

re lovely than all these? And had you but
l the rest of his Service would have seem-
1. To think of him, to speak of him,
1, to praise him; yea, to deny all and
, would have been sweet and pleasant to
you had loved him. It was not God
t your own naughty Hearts that made his
ievous to you, and the Way to Heaven
He told you truly, that his Yoak was easy,
n light, and his Commandments were not
t. 11. 29. 1 *John* 5. 3. They that tried
hem the very Joy and Delight of their
hy could not you do so?

t if the Way to Heaven had been harder
Was not Heaven worth your Labour?
raid of being a loser by it? Could not
our Labour or Sufferings? Doth any re-
ey come to Heaven, that it cost them so
thither? And is not Hell worse than the
to Heaven? Seeing you have chosen Hell
t Labour and Suffering in this Life, you
ur Choice. And seeing you thought not
fe to be worth so much as God required,
accepting thankfully, and minding, and
preferring it before this Life, you have
e for the loss of it but your selves.

enth Excuse. *It was God that made me of
e: He gave me an Appetite to Meat, and
Ease, and Lust: he gave me that Flesh which
then can he condemn me, for living according
which he gave me?*

gave that Appetite to be exercised mode-
the Rule of Reason, for the Preservation
ion of Mankind: But did he not also give
o govern that Appetite? and the Revela-
Will to guide that Reason? He gave you
o be a Servant, and not a Master. Your
shly Appetite without Reason; and there-

 fore

fore God hath put him under you, who have Reason that you should rule him. Will you let your Beast do what he list, and madly run upon whom he list, and say, you do but let him live according to his Nature which God hath given him? Why God that gave him such a Nature, did intend him to be ruled by a higher Nature, even by the Reason which he gave to you: and so he did also by your Flesh and sensual Appetite.

The nineteenth Excuse. *But I lived among so many Baits which enticed this Flesh, that I could not resist them. My Meat was a Snare to me, my Drink a Snare, my Clothes, my House, my Land a Snare, every Beauty that I saw was a Snare: and the better all these were, the stronger was my Snare. If God would not have had my Heart ensnared and drawn from him, he should not have put so many Baits in my way. Yea and they were so near to me, and daily with me, that though I was resolved to forbear them before, yet when they were brought to my hand, I could not forbear.*

Answ. Is this the Thanks that God hath for his Mercies? He sent you all these as Favours from his own hand: he wrote his own Name upon them, that in them you might see his Power, and Wisdom, and Goodness, and so be led up to the Consideration of him, that you might fall in love with himself, who was the Fountain, the Life, the End of all. And do you overlook God in the Creature, and live as without him in the World, and dote upon that which should have drawn you to himself, and then lay the Blame on God? If he send a Sutor to speak to you in his Name, and write you a Love-Letter with his own Hand, will you fall in love with the Messengers or the Letter, and neglect the Sender, and then blame him that wrote his Letter on so fair a Paper, or in so neat a Hand, or that sent it by such a comely Messenger? Certainly, these Excuses are too gross, to take with the wise and righteous God, or to seem sufficient to a well informed Conscience.

2. And

2. And whereas you speak of the Power of these Objects, was there not much more in God, in Christ, in the promised Glory, to have drawn your Heart another Way? Why then did not these take as much with you as the other? You could not choose forsooth, but be enticed with such Baits as were fitted to your sensual Appetite, and such things as a Dog, or a Swine may enjoy as well as a Man: but you could *choose*, when Christ and Glory were offered you: yea you did *choose* to refuse the Offer, and tread them under Feet by your neglect. When Satan set your Cups, and your Harlots, and your Profits before you on one side; did not God set his Favour and everlasting Happiness on the other side? And was it wise or equal Dealing, to prefer your Lusts before that Glory?

3. Moreover, it was not in the Power of any of those Baits to force your Will, or to necessitate you to choose them. They could be but *Baits* to entice you, and it was still in your own Choice, whether you would yield to the Enticement, and choose them or not. Shall every Man be false to God that hath any Bait to entice him from him? will you excuse your Child or Friend, if he would be false to you, upon as great Enticements as these? If a Cup of Drink, or a Whore, or a little Gain, could draw him more than all your Love and Interest, I do not think you would hold him excused.

And whereas you speak of the *nearness* and *continuance* of these Allurements, I would fain know, was not God as *near* you, and *continually* near you, to draw you to himself? Faith might have seen him, though Flesh and Blood cannot. Did he not stand by you when you were in your Cups and lustful Pleasures? Did he not tell you of the Danger, and offer you far better things, if you would obey him and despise those Baits? But you would hearken to none of this; you should have remembred that he stood over you, and was looking on you, and you should have said as *Joseph*,

 Gen.

Gen. 39. 9. *How can I do this great Wickedness, and sin against God?* You had also Scripture near you, and Reason near you, and Conscience near you, as well as the Bait was near you. And therefore this is a vain Excuse.

The twentieth Excuse. *It was God that let loose the Devil to tempt me; and he was too subtile for me to deal with; and therefore what wonder if I sinned and were overcome?*

Answ. 1. He did not let loose the Devil to *constrain* you to Sin. He could but *entice*, and you might choose whether you would yield. The Devil could neither make you sin against your Will, nor yet necessitate you to be willing.

2. You were a sure Friend to Christ that while, that would forsake him as oft as you were tempted by the Devil. Is that a Friend or a Servant worthy to be regarded, that will disobey you, or betray you as oft as he is tempted to it?

3. Will you excuse your Servant if he leave your Work undone, and follow Cards, or Dice, or the Alehouse, and say I was tempted to it by one that was cunninger than I? Shall every Murderer or Thief escape hanging, because the Devil was too cunning for him in his Temptations? Would you have the Jury or the Judg to take this for a good Excuse?

4. And why did you not hearken to God that enticed you the other way? You forget what Helps he afforded you to discover the Wiles of Satan, and to vanquish the Temptation? He *told* you it was an Enemy that tempted you: and would you hearken to an Enemy? He *told* you it was a Dream, a Shadow, a painted Pleasure, a guilded Carcass, a lying Promise, and deceitful Vanity by which you were tempted; and yet would you regard it before your God? He told you that it was your God, your Saviour, your Hope, your everlasting Happiness that the Tempter would beguile you of: And yet would you be beguiled? He told you, and plainly,

plainly, and often told you, that the Temper would lead you to eternal Fire, and undo you everlastingly before you were aware; and that a fatal Hook was covered with that Bait: And yet would you swallow it?

5. It is plain by all this that it was not your natural Weakness of Faculties that caused you to be overcome by the Subtilties of the Devil, as a silly Child is deceived by a crafty Fellow that overwits him: But it was your Carelesness, Inconsiderateness, your sensual Inclinations, and vicious Disposition, that drew you to a wilful Obeying of the Tempter, and rejecting the wholesom Advice of Christ. This therefore is a frivolous Excuse of your Sin.

The one and twentieth Excuse. *But I hope you will not say that all Men have* Free Will! *And if my Will were not free, how could I choose but sin?*

Answ. 1. Your Will was not free from God's Rule and Government. 2. Nor was it free from its natural Inclination to Good in general; for either of these were more properly Slavery. 3. Nor was it free from the Influence of a dark Understanding. 4. Nor free from its own contracted vitious Inclination. 5. Nor freed from the Temptations of the Flesh, the World, and the Devil.

But it was, 1. Free from any natural Determination to Evil, or to any thing that was doubtful. 2. And free from the Coaction or Violence of any. 3. And free from an irresistible Determination of any exteriour Cause, at least ordinarily. So that naturally, as Men, you have the Power or Faculty of determining your own Wills, and by your Wills of ruling your inferiour Faculties in a great measure; yea, of ruling the Senses and the Phantasy it self, which doth so much to dispose of our Understanding. And if your Wills, which are naturally free, are yet so habitually vitious, that they encline you to do evil, that is not an Excuse, but an Aggravation of your Sin. But of this more under the next.

The two and twentieth Excuse. *But I have not Power of my self to do any thing that is good: what can the Creature do? without Christ we can do nothing. It is God that must give me Ability, or I can have none: and if he had given it me, I had not been an Unbeliever or Impenitent. I can no more believe of my self, than I can fulfil the Law of my self.*

Answ. 1. These are the vain Cavils of learned Folly, which God will easily answer in a Word. The Word [Power] is taken in several Senses. Sometime, and most commonly and fitly, for a Faculty or a Strength by which a Man *can* do his Duty if he *will*. This physical Power you have, and the worst of Sinners have while they are Men on Earth. Were they actually willing, they might acceptably perform sincere Obedience; and were they dispositively willing, they might actually believe and will. And thus the Ungodly have Power to believe.

Sometime the word [Power] is taken for Authority or Leave, for legal or civil Power. And thus you have all not only Power or Liberty to believe, but also a Command which makes it your Duty, and a Threatning adjoined, which will condemn you if you do not.

Sometime the Word [Power] is taken ethically, and less properly, for a Disposition, Inclination, Habit, or Freedom from the contrary Habit or Disposition. And in this Sense it's true, that none but the effectually called have a Power to believe. But then observe, 1. That this is but a Moral, less proper, and not a Physical proper Impotency: And therefore *Austin* chuseth rather to say that all Men have *power* to believe, but all have not a *Will*, or *Faith* it self; because we use to difference *Power* from *Willingness*; and *Willingness* actuateth the *Power* which we had before. And therefore our Divines choose rather to call Grace a Habit when they speak exactly, than a Power; and Dr. *Twiss* derides the Arminians for talking of a *Power* subjected in a

Power. 2. Note that this Impotency is but the same thing with your Unwillingness and wilful Blindness in another Word. 3. Note that this Impotency is long of your selves as to the Original, and much more as to the not curing and removing of it. Hath God given you no means towards the Cure of this Disability, which you have neglected? 4. Note that this Impotency is not a just Excuse, but an Aggravation of your Sin. If you were *willing* to be the Servant of Christ, and yet were not able either because he would not accept you, or because of a want of natural Faculties, or because of some other natural Difficulty which the *willingest* Mind could not overcome, this were some Excuse: But to be habitually wilful in refusing Grace, is worse than to be meerly actually unwilling. If a Man have so accustomed himself to Murder, Drunkenness, Stealing or the like Wickedness, so far that he cannot leave it, will you therefore forgive him, or will any Judg or Jury hold him excused? Or rather think him the more unfit for Mercy? 5. Note also that the want of a supernatural Habit, no nor the Presence of the contrary Habit, do not efficiently determine the Will to particular Acts, much less take away its natural Freedom. 6. And that till Habits attain an utter Predominancy, (at least) there is a Power remaining in the Will to resist them, and use Means against them. Though eventually the perverse Inclination may hinder the use of it.

The three and twentieth Excuse. *I have heard from learned Men, that God doth determine all Actions, natural and free, as the first efficient physical immediate Cause: or else nothing could act. And then it was not long of me that I chose forbidden Objects, but of him that irresistibly moved me thereto, and whose Instrument I was.*

Answ. This is a trick of that Wisdom which is Foolishness with God, and to be deceived by vain Philosophy.

1. The

1. The very Principle it ſelf is moſt likely to be falſe, and thoſe that tell you this do err. Much more, I think, may be ſaid againſt it than for it.

2. I am ſure it is either falſe, or irreconcileable with God's Holineſs, and Man's Liberty and Culpability; ſo that its a mad thing to deceive your ſelves with ſuch philoſophical Uncertainties, when the Truth which you oppoſe by it is infallibly certain. That God is not the Author of Sin, but Man himſelf, who is juſtly condemned for it, is undoubtedly true: and would you obſcure ſo clear a Truth, by ſearching into Points beyond humane Reach if not unſound, as you conclude them?

The four and twentieth Excuſe. *But at leaſt, thoſe learned Divines among us that doubt of this, do yet ſay that the Will is neceſſarily and infallibly determined by the practical Underſtanding, and that is as much unreſiſtibly neceſſitated by Objects: and therefore whatever act was done by my Underſtanding or Will, was thus neceſſitated, and I could not help it. They ſay, Liberty is but the Acting of the Faculty agreeably to its Nature: And it was God as Creator that gave* Adam *his Faculties, and God by providential Diſpoſe, that preſented all Objects to him, by which his Underſtanding, and ſo his Will were unavoidably neceſſitated.*

Anſw. This is of the ſame Nature with the former; uncertain, if not certainly falſe. Were this true, for ought we can ſee, it would lay all the Sin and Miſery of this World on God, as the unreſiſtible neceſſitating Cauſe; which becauſe we know infallibly to be falſe, we have no reaſon to take ſuch Principles to be true which infer it. The Underſtanding doth not by a neceſſary Efficiency determine the Will, but morally; or rather, is regularly a Condition or neceſſary Antecedent, without which it may not determine it ſelf. Yea the Will by commanding the Senſe and Phantaſy, doth much to determine the Underſtanding. As the Eye is not neceſſary to my *going*, but to my *going right*, ſo is not the Underſtanding's Guidance neceſſary to

my

my *willing*, (there the simple Apprehension may suffice) but to my *right willing*. There are other ways of determining the Will. Or if the Understanding did determine the Will efficiently and necessarily, it is not every act of the Understanding that must do it. If it be so, when it saith, This *must* be done, and saith it importunately; yet not when it only saith, This may be done, or you may venture on it, which is the common part which it hath in Sin.

I am not pleased that these curious Objections fall in the Way, nor do I delight to put them into vulgar Heads; but finding many young Scholars and others that have conversed with them, assaulted with these Temptations, I thought meet to give a Touch, and but a Touch, to take them out of their Way: As Mr. *Fenner* hath done more fully in the Preface to his *Hidden Manna*, on this last point, to which I refer you. I only add this.

The Will of Man in its very Dominion doth bear God's Image. It is a self-determining Power, though it be *biassed* by *Habits*, and *needs* a *Guide*. As the Heart and Vital Spirits by which it acteth, are to the rest of the Body, so is *it* to the Soul. The Light of Nature hath taught all the World to carry the Guilt of every Crime to the *Will* of Man, and there to leave it. Upon this all Laws and Judgments are grounded. From Ignorance and intellectual Weakness, Men commonly fetch Excuses for their Faults; but from the Will they are aggravated. If we think it strange that Man's Will should be the first Cause, so much as of a sinful *Mode*, and answer all occurring Objections: it may suffice that we are certain the Holy Majesty is not the Author of Sin; and he is able to make all this as plain as the Sun, and easily answer all these vain Excuses, though we should be unable. And if we be much ignorant of the Frame and Motions of our own Souls, and especially of that high self-determining Principle, free-Will, the great Spring of our Actions, and the curious Engine by which God

doth

doth *sapientially* govern the World, it is no wonder, considering that the Soul can know it self but by Reflection, and God gave us a Soul to *use*, rather than to know it self; and to know its Qualities and Operations, rather than its Essence.

The five and twentieth Excuse. *No Man can be saved, nor avoid any Sin, nor believe in Christ, but those whom God hath predestinated thereto. I was under an irreversible Sentence before I was born: and therefore I do nothing but what I was predestinated to do; and if God decreed not to save me, how could I help it?*

Answ. 1. God's Judgments are more plain, but his Decrees or secret Purposes are mysterious: And to darken Certainties, by having recourse to Points obscure, is no part of Christian Wisdom. God told you your Duty in his Word, and on what Terms you must be judged to Life or Death; hither should you have recourse for Direction, and not to the unsearchable Mysteries of his *Mind*.

2. God decreeth not to condemn any but for Sin. Sin, I say, is the Cause of that Condemnation, though not of his Decree.

3. God's Decrees are Acts Immanent in himself, and make no change on you, and therefore do not necessitate you to sin, any more than his Fore-knowledg doth. For both cause only a necessity of Consequence, which is Logical, as the Divines on both sides do confess. And therefore this no more caused you to sin, than if there had been no such Decree. And it's a Doubt whether that Decree be not negative; a willing Suspending of the Divine Will, as to evil; or at most a Purpose to permit it.

The six and twentieth Excuse. *If it be no more, yet doth it make my Perdition unavoidable; for even God's Foreknowledg doth so; for if he foreknow it, all the World cannot hinder it from coming to pass.*

Answ. Must God either be ignorant of what you will do, or else be the Cause of it? If you foreknow

that

that the Sun will rise to morrow, that doth not cause it to rise. If you foreknow that one Man will murder another, you are not the Cause of it by foreknowing it. So is it here.

The seven and twentieth Excuse. *God might have hindred my Sin and Damnation if he would.*

Answ. And will you wilfully sin, and think to escape because God doth not hinder you? The Prince that makes a Law against Murder, could lock you up, and keep you from being a Murderer. But are you excusable if he do not? We are certain that God could have hindered all the Sin and Death, and Confusion, and Misery that is in the Word: and we are as certain that he doth not hinder it (but by forbidding it, and giving Men means against it:) and we are certain that he is Just, and Good, and Wise in all, and not bound to hinder it: And what his Reasons are, you may better know hereafter: In the mean time, you had been better have looked to your own Duty.

The eight and twentieth Excuse. *How could I be saved if Christ did not die for me? He died but for his Elect; and none could be saved without his Death.*

Answ. He *did* die for you, and for more than his Elect, though he absolutely purposed only their Salvation. Your Sins crucified him, and your Debt lay upon him; and he so far ransomed you, that nothing but your wilful Refusal of the Benefits could have condemned you.

The nine and twentieth Excuse. *It was* Adam's *Sin that brought me into this Depravedness of* Will, *which I can neither cure, nor could prevent.*

Answ. 1. If *Adam* cast away his Holiness, he could no more convey that to us which he cast away, than a Nobleman that is a Traitor, can convey his lost Inheritance or Honours to his Son.

2. You perish not only for your Original Sin, but for rejecting the recovering Mercy of the Redeemer: you might have had Christ and Life in him for the accepting.

The

The thirtieth Excuse. *God will require no more than he gives. He gave me not Grace to repent and believe; and without his Gift I could not have it.*

Answ. 1. God will justly require more than he giveth; that is, the improvement of his Gifts, as *Mat.* 25. shews. He gave *Adam* but a *Power* to persevere, and not *actual Perseverance:* Yet did he justly punish him for want of the Act; even for not using by his own Wll the Power which he had given him.

2. It is long of your self if God did not give you Grace to believe: It was because you wilfully refused some preparatory Grace. Christ found you at a great distance from him, and he gave you Grace sufficient to have brought you *nearer* to him than you were; you had Grace sufficient to have made you better than you were, and restrained many Sins, and brought you to the means, when you turned your back on them: tho this were not *sufficient* to cause you to *believe*, it was *sufficient* to have brought you *nearer* to *believing*; and through your own wilfulness, became *not effectual*; even as *Adam* had *sufficient* Grace to have stood, which was *not effectual.* So that you had not only Christ offered to you, if you would but accept him; but you had daily and precious Helps and Means, to have cured your Wills, and caused you to accept him; for neglect of which, and so for not believing, and so for all your other Sins, you justly perish.

The one and thirtieth Excuse. *Alas, Man is a Worm, a dry Leaf!* Job 13. 25. *a silly foolish Creature, and therefore his Actions be not regardable, nor deserve so great a Punishment.*

Answ. Though he be a Worm, and as nothing to God, and foolish by Sin, yet he is naturally so noble a Creature, that the Image of God was on him, *Gen.* 12. 25. and 5. 1. *James* 3. 9. and the World made his Servants, and Angels his Attendants, *Heb.* 1. 14. so noble that Christ died for him, God takes special care of him; he is capable of knowing and enjoying God, and Heaven is not thought too good for him if he will obey. And he that is capable of so great Good, must be capable of as great Evil, and his Ways not to be so overlooked by that God that hath undertaken to be his Governour. When it tendeth to Infidelity, the Devil will teach you to debase Man, even lower than God would do.

The two and thirtieth Excuse. *Sin is no* Being: *and shall Men be damned for that which is nothing?*

Answ. 1. It is such a *Mode* as deformeth God's Creature. It is a moral Being. It is a Relation of our Actions and Hearts to God's Will and Law.

2. They that say, Sin is nothing, say Pain and Loss is nothing too. You shall therefore be paid with one nothing for another. Make light of your Misery, and say, it is nothing, as you did of your Sin.

3. Will you take this for a good Excuse from your Children or Servants, if they abuse you? or from a Thief or a Murderer? shall he escape by telling the Judg that his Sin was *nothing?* Or rather have Death, which is nothing, as the just Reward of it?

The three and thirtieth Excuse. *But Sin is a transient Thing. At least it doth God no harm, and therefore why should he do us so much harm for it?*

Answ. 1. It hurts not God, because he is above hurt. No thanks to you if he be out of your reach. 2. You may *wrong* him, when you cannot *hurt* him. And the *Wrong* deserves as much as you can bear. If a Traitor endeavour the Death of the Prince in vain, his Endeavour deserves Death, though he never *hurt* him. You despise God's Law and Authority; you cause the Blaspheming of his Name, *Rom.* 2. 24. He calls it a Pressing him as a Cart is pressed with Sheaves, *Amos* 2. 13. and a Grieving of him.

3. And you wrong his Image, his Church, the publick Good, and the Souls of others.

The four and thirtieth Excuse. *But God's Nature is so good and merciful, that sure he will not damn his own Crea-*

Answ. 1. A merciful Judg will hang a Man for a Fault against Man: By proportion then what is due for Sin against God?

2. All the Death and Calamity which you see in the World, comes from the Anger of this merciful God: why then may not future Misery come from it?

3. God knoweth his own Mercy better than you do; and he hath told you how far it shall extend.

4. He is infinitely merciful; but it is to the Heirs of Mercy, not to the final Rejecters of his Mercy.

5. Hath not God been merciful to thee in bearing with thee so long, and offering thee Grace in the Blood of Christ, till thou didst wilfully reject it? Thou wilt confess to thy everlasting Wo that God was merciful; had he not been so merciful, thou wouldst not have been so miserable for rejecting it.

The five and thirtieth Excuse. *I would not so torment mine Enemy my self.*

Answ. No reason you should. Is it all one to wrong you, and to wrong the God of Heaven? God is the only Judg of his own Wrongs.

The sixth and thirtieth Excuse. *All Men are Sinners; and I was but a Sinner.*

Answ. All were not impenitent, unbelieving, rebellious Sinners, and therefore all are not unpardoned, condemned Sinners. All did not live after the Flesh, and refuse to the last to be converted as you did. God will teach you better to difference between Sinners and Sinners.

The seven and thirtieth Excuse. *But if Christ have satisfied for my Sins, and died for me, then how can I justly suffer for the same Sins? will God punish one Sin twice?*

Answ. 1. Christ suffered for Man in the Nature of Man; but not in your Person, nor you in him. It was not you that provided the Price, but God himself: Christ was not Man's Delegate in satisfying, and therefore received not his Instructions from us, nor did

it

rms, but his own. It was not the *same* ie Law threatned, that Christ underwent: the Damnation of the Sinner himself, and ring of another for him; it cannot there- ; but on Christ's own Terms. He died ut with this intent, that for all that if thou hou shalt die thy self. It is therefore no e to die, for it was not thou that diedst Christ will take it for no wrong to him: dg thee to that Death. It is for refusing died for thee, that thou must perish for

and thirtieth Excuse. *But I did not refuse eved and trusted in him to the last; and repent- s, though I sometime was overtaken with*

this been true, thy Sin would not have hee. But there is no mocking God. He hee then thy naked Heart, and convince it thought they believed and repented, that did not. By thy Works also will this be hat is, by the main bent and scope of thy 25. throughout, and *Jam.* 2.

and thirtieth Excuse. *I did many good I hope God will set those against my evil*

good Works were thy Sins, because in- re not good, being not done in sincerity of d. The best Man's Works have some In- ch nothing can cleanse but the Blood of thou hast made light of, and therefore . If all thy Life had been spent in per- cept one day, they would not make satis- Sins of that Day. For they are but part Wo to him that hath no better a Savi- nt, than his own good Works.

Excuse. *I lived in Poverty and Misery on refore I hope I have had my Sufferinghere,*

and

and ſhall not ſuffer in this World and another too.

1. By that Rule all poor Men and Murderers, and Thieves that are tormented and hanged, ſhould be ſaved. But as Godlineſs hath the Promiſe of this Life and that to come, ſo Impenitency and Wickedneſs hath the Threatning of this Life and that to come.

2. The Devils and the damned have ſuffered much more than you already; and yet they are never the nearer a Deliverance. When thou haſt ſuffered ten thouſand Years, thy Pain will be never the nearer an end. How then can a little Miſery on Earth prevent it? Alas, poor Soul, theſe are but the Foretaſts and Beginnings of thy Sorrow. Nothing but Pardon through the Blood of Chriſt could have prevented thy Condemnation; and that thou rejectedſt by Infidelity and Impenitency. *His* Sufferings would have ſaved thee, if thou hadſt not refuſed him; but all thy own Sufferings will yield thee no Relief.

So much for the anſwering of the *vain Excuſes* which poor Sinners are ready to make for themſelves; wherein I have been ſo large, as that this part I confeſs is diſproportionable to the reſt: but it was for theſe two Reaſons.

1. That poor careleſs Souls might ſee the Vanity of ſuch Defences; and conſider if ſuch a Worm as I can eaſily confute them, how eaſily and how terribly will they be all anſwered by their Judg?

2. I did it the rather, that godly Chriſtians might the better underſtand how to deal with theſe vain Excuſes when they meet with them: which will be daily, if they deal with Men in this ſad Condition.

X. We have done with that part of the Judgment which conſiſteth in the Exploration or Trial of the Cauſe: we now come to that which is the Concluſion and Conſummation of all; and that is, to ſhew you *what the Sentence will be, and on whom.*

And

And for this, we must go strait to the Word of God for our Light, it being impossible for any Man to have any particular Knowledg of it, if Christ had not there revealed it unto us. Indeed almost all the World do acknowledg a Life after this, where it shall go well with the Good, and ill with the bad. But who shall be then accounted *righteous*, and who *unrighteous*, and on what Terms and Grounds, by whom they shall be judged, and to what Condition, they know not.

The Sentence in Judgment will be, 1. Either on those that never had Means to know Christ. 2. Or on those that had.

1. For the former, as it less concerneth us to enquire of their Case, so it is more obscurely revealed to us in the Scripture. It is certain that they shall be judged according to their Use of the Means which they had, *Rom.* 2. 11, 12, 13, 14, 15, 16. and the Talents which they received, *Mat.* 25. But that it ever falleth out that he that hath but the one Talent of natural Helps, doth improve it to Salvation; or that ever they who knew not Christ, are justified and saved without that Knowledg, (being at Age and Use of Reason) I find not in the Scriptures. I find indeed that [as many as have sinned without Law, shall also perish without Law: and as many as have sinned *in* the Law, shall be judged *by* the Law, *Rom.* 2. 12. but not that any are justified by the Works of Nature, such as are here said to be *without* Law.] I find also, that [They have the Work of the Law written in their Hearts, their Conscience also bearing witness, and their Thoughts the mean while accusing, or else excusing one another, in the Day *when* God shall judg the Secrets of Men by Jesus Christ, according to the Gospel] *Rom.* 2. 15, 16. And I believe it is a *just Excuse*, and not an *unjust* which is here meant. But it will be but an *Excuse* so far as they were guiltless : and that will be but *in tanto*, and not *in toto*, in part only ; and so not a full Justification. A Heathen's Conscience may excuse him from those Sins which he was

never

never guilty of; but not from all. But no more of them.

2. The Case of those that have had the Gospel, is more plainly opened to us in God's Word. Their *Sentence* is opened in many Places of Scripture, but most fully in *Matth.* 25. whence we will now collect it.

There we find that Jesus Christ the Redeemer, as King of the World, shall sit in Judgment on all Men at the last; and shall separate them one from another, as a Shepherd divideth the Sheep from the Goats, and so shall pass the final Sentence. This Sentence is twofold, according to the different Condition of them that are judged. To them on the right Hand, there is a Sentence of Justification, and Adjudication to everlasting Glory: To them on the left Hand, there is a Sentence of Condemnation to everlasting Punishment.

The Sentence on each of these containeth both the State which they are judged to, and the Reason or Cause of the Judgment to that State. For as God will not judg any to Life or Death without just Cause, so he will publish this Cause in his Sentence, as it is the manner of Judges to do. If you say, *Christ will not use a Voice*; let it satisfy, that though we know not the manner, yet if he do it but by mental Discovery, as he shews Men *what* shall everlastingly befal them, so he will shew them *why* it shall so befal them.

1. The *Sentence* on them on the *right* Hand, will contain, 1. Their Justification and Adjudication to *Blessedness*, and that both as generally denominated, and as particularly determined and described. 2. And the Cause of this Judgment.

1. In general they shall be pronounced *Blessed*. Satan would have had them cursed and miserable: the Law did curse them to Misery; many a fearful Thought hath possessed their own Breasts, lest they should prove at last accursed and miserable: but now they

hear

rary from their Judg. All the Promiſes
could not perfectly overcome thoſe their
e comfortable Words of the Miniſters
could not perfectly ſubdue them; all the
of God in Chriſt did not perfectly ſubdue
w they are vanquiſhed all for ever. He
heard his Redeemer in Judgment call him
ver fear being *curſed* more. For he that
, ſhall be *bleſſed* indeed.

iption of their Bleſſedneſs followeth,
Kingdom prepared for you from the Founda-
rld. And alſo they are called *Bleſſed*
Here is the Fountain of their Bleſſedneſs,
and the State of their Bleſſedneſs in being
for I ſuppoſe they are called *the Bleſſed of*
th becauſe the Father bleſſeth them, that
m Happy, and becauſe theſe bleſſed Ones
r's *own.* And ſo Chriſt will publiſh it to
Judgment, that he came to glorify the
will proclaim him the principal Efficient,
End of his Work of Redemption, and the
f his Saints; and that himſelf is (as Me-
e *Way* to the Father. It is the Father that
ingdom for them, and *from the Foundation*
repared it; both for [them] as *choſen ones,*
as *future Believers and righteous Ones.* It is
dom, partly in reſpect to God the King,
ory we ſhall partake in our Places; and
horically, from the Dignity of our Condi-
o it is that our ſelves are ſaid to be made
. 6. and 5. 1. 1 *Pet.* 2. 9. and not that
erly Kings; for then we muſt have Sub-
ſt be governed by us.

ſee their Bleſſedneſs in the Fountain, End
Dignity. As to the receptive Act on
is expreſſed by two Words; one ſignifying
trance on it, *Come:* the other their *Poſ-*
: That is, poſſeſs it as given by the Fa-

ther, and Redeemed by the Son, and hold it in this Tenure for ever.

The true Believer was convinced in this Life, that indeed there was no true Bleſſedneſs, but this Enjoyment of God in the Kingdom of Heaven. The Lord revealed this to his Heart by his Word and Spirit: And therefore he contemned the ſeeming Happineſs on Earth, and laid up for himſelf a Treaſure in Heaven, and made him Friends with the Mammon of Unrighteouſneſs, and ventured all his Hope in this Veſſel. And now he findeth the Wiſdom of that Choice in a rich Return. God made him ſo *wiſe* a Merchant as to ſell all for this Pearl of greateſt Price: and therefore now he ſhall find the Gain. As there is no other true Happineſs but God in Glory; ſo is there nothing more *ſutable* and *welcome* to the true Believer. O how welcome will the Face of that God be, whom he *loved*, *ſought*, *longed* and *waited* for! How welcome will that Kingdom be which he lived in *hope* of, which he parted with all for, and ſuffered for in the Fleſh! How glad will he be to ſee the bleſſed Face of his Redeemer, who by his manifold Grace hath brought him unto this! I leave the believing Soul to think of it, and to make it the daily matter of his delightful Meditation; what an unconceivable Joy in one Moment, will this Sentence of Chriſt will fill his Soul with? Undoubtedly it is now quite paſt our Comprehenſion; though our imperfect Forethoughts of it may well make our Lives a continual Feaſt.

Were it but our Juſtification from the Accuſations of Satan, who would have us condemned either as *Sinners* in general, or as impenitent, unbelieving Rebels, againſt him that redeemed us, in *ſpecial*, it would lift up the Heads of the Saints in that Day: After all the Fears of our own Hearts, and the ſlanderous Accuſations of Satan and the World, That we were either impenitent Infidels or Hypocrites, Chriſt will then juſtify us and pronounce us *righteous*. So much for the *Condition to which* they are judged.

2. The

ſon or Cauſe of this Juſtification of the n us both, 1. In a general Denomination, particular Deſcription. 1. In general, ney were *righteous*, as is evident, *Mat.* 25. *eous ſhall go into Life everlaſting.* And in- Buſineſs of every juſt Judg to juſtify the nd condemn the Unrighteous. And ſhall of all the Earth judg righteouſly? *Gen.* makes Men righteous before he judges d judgeth them righteous *becauſe* they are abominateth that Man who ſaith to the Thou art wicked; or to the Wicked, nteous; who juſtifieth the Wicked and he Righteous, will certainly never do ſo

will juſtify them that are Sinners, but not ccuſation *that they are Sinners*, but againſt on, that *they are guilty of Puniſhment for* is, becauſe he firſt made them juſt; and by pardoning their Sin, through the Blood

ue alſo, that he will juſtify thoſe that but not thoſe that *are wicked:* but Judg- them as Death leaveth them, and he will n for wicked, that are ſanctified and heir former Wickedneſs. So that Chriſt on them before he juſtify them againſt the ng Sinners in general; and he will firſt h, Repentance and new Obedience, be- uſtify them againſt the Charge of being nfidels or Hypocrites, and conſequently and doubly guilty of Damnation. This teouſneſs he will firſt *give* Men, and ſo m juſt, before he will *declare* it, and *ſen-*

ſon of the Sentence, particularly de- om their Faith and Love to Chriſt, ex- r Obedience, Self-denial, and forſaking all for him. *For I was hungry and ye fed me; I was thirsty and ye gave me drink; I was a Stranger and ye took me in; naked and ye clothed me: I was sick and ye visited me: I was in Prison and ye came to me. Verily I say unto you, inasmuch as ye have done it to one of the least of these my Brethren, ye have done it unto me*, Mat. 25. 35 to 41. Here is, 1. The causal Conjuction *for*. 2. And the Cause or Reason it self.

Concerning both which, observe. 1. How it is that Man's Obedience and Self-denial is the Reason and Cause of his Justification. 2. Why it is that God will have the Reason or Cause thus declared in the Sentence.

For the first, observe that it's one thing to give a Reason of the Sentence, and another thing to express the *Cause* of the *Benefit given* us by the Promise, and *judged* to us by the *Sentence*. Man's Obedience was no proper Cause why God did in this Life *give* Pardon of Sin to us, or a Right to Glory, much less of his giving Christ to die for us. And therefore as to our constitutive Justification at our Conversion, we must not *say* or *think* that God doth justify us, for, or *because* of any Works of our Obedience, legal or evangelical. But when God hath so justified us, when he comes to give a Reason of his Sentence in Judgment, he may and will fetch that Reason partly from our Obedience, or our Performance of the Conditions of the new Covenant. For as in this Life, we had a Righteousness consisting in free Pardon of all Sin through the Blood of Christ, and a Righteousness consisting in our personal Performance of the Conditions of the Promise, which giveth that Pardon and continueth it to us:

in *James* his ſenſe, *James* 2. 24. ſo accordingly a double Reaſon will be aſſigned of our ſentential Juſtification; one from our Pardon by Chriſt's Blood and Merits, which will prove our Right to Impunity and to Glory; the other from our own Faith and holy Obedience, which will prove our Right to that Pardon through Chriſt, and to the free Gift of a Right to Glory: and ſo this laſt is to be pleaded in Subordination to the former. For Chriſt is become the Author of eternal Salvation to all them that obey him, *Heb.* 5. 9. He therefore that will be ſaved, muſt have a *Chriſt* to ſave him as the Author, and an *Obedience* to that Chriſt as the Condition of that Salvation; and conſequently both muſt be declared in the Judgment.

The Reaſon why the Judg doth mention our good Works rather than our believing, may be becauſe thoſe holy ſelf-denying Expreſſions of Faith and Love to Chriſt do contain or certainly imply Faith in them, as the Life of the Tree is in the Fruit: but Faith doth contain our Works of Obedience but only as their Cauſe. The Works alſo are a Part of the perſonal Righteouſneſs which is to be enquired after, that is, we ſhall not be judged righteous, meerly becauſe we have believed, but alſo becauſe we have added to our Faith Vertue, and have improved our Talents, and have loved Chriſt to the hazard of all for his ſake. For it is not only or principally for the Goodneſs of the Work conſidered in it ſelf, or the Good that is done by it to the Poor; but it is as theſe Works did expreſs our Faith and Love to Chriſt by doing him the moſt coſtly and hazardous Service; that by Faith we could ſee Chriſt in a poor Beggar or a Priſoner, and could love Chriſt in *theſe* better than our worldly Goods or Liberit is the Business of that Day, not only to glorify God's meer Love and Mercy, but eminently to glorify his remunerative Justice; and not only to express his Love to the Elect, as such, but to express his Love to them as *faithful* and *obedient*, and such as have denied all for Christ, and loved God above all; and to shew his Justice to Men, and Faithfulness in fulfilling all his Promises, and also his Holiness, in the high Estimation of the Holiness of his People. I shall express this in the Words of a Learned Divine (Dr. *Twiss* against Mr. *Cotton*, pag. 40.) *Was there no more in God's Intention when he elected some, than the Manifestation of the Riches of his glorious Grace? Did not God purpose also to manifest the Glory of his remunerative Justice? Is it not undeniable that God will bestow Salvation on all his Elect, (of ripe Years) by way of Reward, and Crown of Righteousness, which God the righteous Judg will give?* 2 Tim. 4. 2 Thess. 1. *It is great pity this is not considered, as usually it is not, especially for the momentous Consequence thereof in my Judgment.* So far he.

So much of the Sentence of Justification which shall be passed by Christ at Judgment upon the Righteous.

2. We are next to consider of the Sentence of Condemnation which shall then by Christ be passed on the Unrighteous. Which is delivered to us by Christ, *Mat.* 25. in the same Order as the former.

The Sentence containeth, 1. The Condemnation it self 2. The Reason or Cause of it.

The Condemnation expresseth the Misery which they are judged to. 1. Generally in the Denomination, *Cursed.* 2. Particularly by Description of their cursed State.

To be *cursed*, is to be a People destinated and adjudged to utter Unhappiness, to all kind of Misery without remedy.

2. Their *cursed* Condition is described in the next Words, *Depart from me into everlasting Fire prepared for the*

1. *Depart:* From whom? from the God that made them in his Image; from the Redeemer that bought them by the Price of his Blood, and offered to save them freely, for all their Unworthiness, and many a time intreated them to accept his Offer, that their Souls might live: From the Holy Ghost, the Sanctifier and Comforter of the Faithful, who strove with their Hearts, till they quenched and expelled him. O sad *Departing!* who would not then choose rather to *depart* from all the Friends he had in the World, and from any thing imaginable; from his Life, from himself, if it were possible, than from Christ? *Depart:* from what? why from the Presence of the Judg, from all farther Hopes of *Salvation* for ever, from all possibility of ever being saved, and living in the joyful Inheritance of the Righteous. *Depart:* Not from God's Essential Presence, for that will be with them to their everlasting Misery, but from the Presence of his Grace in that Measure as they enjoyed it. *Depart:* Not from your fleshly Pleasures, and Honours, and Profits of the World; these were all gone and past already: and there was no farther need to bid them *depart* from these: Houses and Lands were gone. Mirth and Recreations were gone. Their sweet Morsels and Cups were gone. All the Honour that Men could give them was gone before they were set at Christ's Bar to be judged. But from all Expectations of ever enjoying these again, or ever *tasting* their former Delights; from these they must depart: not from their *Sin*, for that will go with them; but the Liberty of committing that part of it which was sweet to them, as Gluttony, Drunkenness, Whoredom, Idleness, and all Voluptuousness; from these they must *depart*. But this is consequential; it is Christ and the Possibility of Salvation, that they are sentenced to *depart* from.

But *whither* must they *depart?* 1. Into Fire. 2. Into *that* Fire which was prepared for the Devil and his Angels. 3. Into everlasting Fire.

1. Not into a *purifying*, but a *tormenting* Fire. Whether elementary or not; whether properly or metaphorically called *Fire*, let us not vainly trouble our selves to enquire. It is enough to know, that as Fire is one of the most grievous Tormentors of the Flesh, so grievous will be those infernal Torments to the whole Man, Soul and Body; such as is most fitly represented to us under the Notion of *Fire*, and of *Burning*. It is easy for a secure unbelieving Soul to read and hear of it; but Wo and ten thousand Woes to them that must endure it! In this Life they had their good things, when it went harder as to the Flesh with better Men; but now they are tormented, when the Godly are comforted, as *Luke* 16. 25.

2. But why is it called *a Fire prepared for the Devil and his Angels?* 1. What is this Devil that hath Angels? 2. Who are his Angels? 3. When was it prepared for them? 4. Was it not also prepared for wicked Men? To these in order.

1. It seems by many Passages in Scripture, that there is an Order among Spirits both good and bad; and that there is one Devil that is the Prince over the rest.

2. It seems therefore that it's the rest of the evil Spirits, that are called *his Angels*. And some think that the Wicked who served him in this Life, shall be numbred with his Angels in the Life to come. Indeed the Apostle calls him *the God of this World*, 2 Cor. 4. 4. as is ordinarily judged by Expositors; and *the Prince of the Power of the Air, the Spirit that now worketh in the Children of Disobedience*, Eph. 2. 2. And he calleth false seducing Teachers *the Ministers of Satan*, 2 Cor. 11. 15. But that wicked Men are here meant as part of his Angels, is not clear.

3. If it be the Preparation of God's Purpose that is here meant, then it was from Eternity: but if it be any Commination of God as Ruler of the Angels, then was this Fire prepared for them conditionally, from the

the beginning of that Commination, and was *due* to them at their Fall.

4. It ſeems that the Reaſon why here is no mention of preparing Hell-fire for the Wicked, but only for the Devils, is not becauſe indeed it *was not* prepared alſo for the Wicked ; but to note that it is the Torment which was *firſt* prepared for, or aſſigned to the Devils, thereby ſhewing the greatneſs of the Miſery of the Wicked, that the Devil and his Angels muſt be their Companions : Though ſome think, as is ſaid before, that the Reaſon why wicked Men are not mentioned here, is, becauſe they are part of the Angels of the Devil, and ſo included. And ſome think it is purpoſely to manifeſt God's general Love to Mankind, that prepared not Hell *for them*, but they caſt themſelves into the Hell prepared for the Devils. But the firſt ſeems to be the true ſenſe.

And how apparently Righteous are the Judgments of the Lord! that thoſe Men who would here entertain the Devil into their Hearts and daily Familiarity, ſhould be then entertained by him into *his* Place of Torments, and there remain for ever in his Society! Though few entertained him into viſible Familiarity with their Bodies as Witches do, who ſo make him their *Familiar* : yet all wicked Men do entertain him into more full and conſtant Familiarity with their Souls than theſe Witches do with their Bodies ; how *familiar* is he in Thoughts, to fill them with Vanity, Luſt or Revenge ! How *familiar* is he in their Hearts, to fill them with Covetouſneſs, Malice, Pride, or the like Evils! and to baniſh all Thoughts of returning to God, and to quench every Motion that tendeth to their Recovery! How *familiar* is he with them, even when they ſeem to be worſhipping God in the publick Aſſemblies, ſtealing the Word out of their Hearts, filling them with vain and wandring Thoughts, blinding their Minds that they cannot underſtand the plaineſt words that we are able to ſpeak to them, and filling them with a proud

Rebellion against the Direction of their Teachers, and an obstinate Refusal to be ruled by them, be the Matter never so necessary to their own Salvation? How *familiar* are these evil Spirits in their Houses, filling them with Ignorance, Worldliness and Ungodliness, and turning out God's Service, so that they do not pray together once in a Day, or perhaps at all! How *familiarly* doth Satan use their Tongues, in Cursing, Swearing, Lying, Ribaldry, Backbiting or Slandring! And is it not just with God to make these Fiends their *Familiars* in Torment, with whom they entertained such *Familiarity* in Sin? As Christ with all the blessed Angels and Saints will make but one Kingdom or Family, and shall live altogether in perpetual Delights; so the Devil and all his hellish Angels and wicked Men shall make but one Houshold, and shall live altogether in perpetual Misery. O poor Sinners, you are not troubled now at his Presence and Power in your Hearts! but will you not then be troubled at his Presence and tormenting Power? As long as you do not *see* him, let him do what he will with you, it grieves you little or nothing at all; but what will you say when you *must see* him, and abide with him for ever? O Sirs, his Name is *easily* heard, but his Company will be terrible to the stoutest Heart alive. He sheweth you a smiling Face when he tempteth you, but he hath a grimmer Face to shew you, when Temptations have conquered you, and Torments must succeed. As those that write of Witches, say, he appeareth at first to them in some comely tempting Shape, till he have them fast tied to him; and then he beats them, and affrights them, and seldom appears to them but in some ugly Hew. Believe it, poor Sinners, you do not hear or see the worst of him, when you are merry about your sinful Pleasures, and rejoicing in your Hopes of the Commodities or Preferments of the World: he hath another kind of Voice which you must hear, and another Face to shew you, that will make you know a *little*

better

better whom you had to do with! You would be afraid now to meet him in the Dark: what will you be to live with him in everlasting Darkneſs? Then you will know who it was that you entertained and obeyed, and plaid with in your Sins.

3. And as the Text tells us, that it is *a Fire prepared for the Devil and his Angels:* So it telleth us, that it is *an everlaſting Fire.* It had a Beginning, but it ſhall have no End. If theſe Wretches would have choſen the Service of God, they would have met with no Difficulty or Trouble, but what would have had a ſpeedy End. Poverty and Injuries would have had an End: Scorns and Abuſes would have had an End: Faſting, Humiliation, Sorrow for Sin, watching and fighting againſt our ſpiritual Enemies, would all have had an End. But to avoid theſe, they choſe that Eaſe, that Pleaſure, which hath brought them to that Torment which *never* will have end. I have ſaid ſo much of theſe things already in my Book called *the Saints Reſt*, that I will now ſay but this much. It is one of the Wonders of the World, how Men that do believe, or think they do believe this Word of Chriſt to be true, that *the Wicked ſhall go into everlaſting Fire*, can yet venture on Sin ſo boldly, and live in it ſo fearleſly, or ſleep quietly till they are out of this unſpeakable Danger! Only the commonneſs of it, and the known Wickedneſs of Man's Heart, doth make this leſs wonderful. And were there nothing elſe to convince us that Sinners are mad and dead as to ſpiritual Things, this were enough; that even the greateſt Pleaſures or Profits of the World, or the moſt enticing Baits that the Devil can offer them, ſhould once prevail with

care not what Ministers say, or what such as I say, yet will you soberly read now and then this 25*th* Chapter of *Matthew*, and regard what is told you by him that must be your Judg! and now and then bethink your selves soberly, whether these are Matters for wise Men to make light of; and what it is to be *everlastingly in Heaven, or in Hell-fire*.

2. We have seen what is the Penalty contained in the Sentence against the Ungodly: The next thing that the Text directs us to, is the Cause or Reason of the Sentence, *ver*. 42. *For I was hungry, and ye gave me no Meat*, &c. The Reason is not given expresly, either for their Sin against the Law of Works, that is, because they were Sinners, and not perfectly *innocent*; nor yet from their Unbelief, which is the great Sin against the Law of Grace: But it is given from their not expressing their Faith and Love to Christ in Works of Mercy and Self-denial. And why is this so?

1. We must not suppose that these Words of Christ do express the *whole* judicial Process in every Point; but the chief Parts. It is supposed that all Men are convicted of being Sinners against the perfect Law of the Creator, and that they are guilty of Death for that Sin; and that there is no way but by Christ to obtain Deliverance. But because all this must be acknowledged by the Righteous themselves, as well as by the Wicked; therefore Christ doth not mention this, but that only which is the turning Point or Cause in the Judgment. For it is not all Sinners that shall be finally condemned, but all impenitent, unbelieving Sinners, who have rebelled finally against their Redeemer.

2. And the Reason why Faith it self is not expressed, is, 1. Because it is clearly implied, and so is Love to Christ as Redeemer; in that they should have relieved *Christ* himself in his Members: That is, as it's expressed, *Mat*. 10. 42. they should have received a Prophet in the

Name

Name of a Prophet, and a Disciple in the Name of a Disciple; all should be done for Christ's sake, which could not be, unless they believed in him, and loved him. 2. Also because that the bare Act of Believing is not all that Christ requireth to a Man's final Justification and Salvation; but holy self-denying Obedience must be added. And therefore this is given as the Reason of their Condemnation that they did not so obey.

We must observe also, that Christ here putteth the special for the general; that is, one way of self-denying Obedience and Expression of Love, instead of such Obedience in general: For all Men have not Ability to relieve those in misery, being perhaps some of them poor themselves. But all have that Love and Self-denial, which will some way express it self. And all have Hearts and a Disposition to do thus, if they had Ability; without such a Disposition none can be saved.

It is the fond Conceit of some, that if they have any Love to the Godly, or wish them well, it is enough to prove them happy. But Christ here purposely lets us know that whoever doth not love him at so high a rate, as that he can part with his Substance or any thing in the World, to those Uses which he shall require them, even to relieve his Servants in want and Sufferings for the Master's sake, that Man is none of Christ's Disciple, nor will be owned by him at the last.

XI. The next Point that we come to, is to shew you the *Properties* of this Sentence at Judgment.

When Man had broken the Law of his Creator at the first, he was liable to the Sentence of Death, and God presently sat in Judgment on him, and sentenced him to some part of the Punishment which he had deserved; but upon the Interposition of the Son, he before the rest, resolved on a Way that might tend to his Recovery; and Death is due yet to every Sinner for every Sin which he commits, till a Pardon do acquit him.

him. But this Sentence which will paſs on Sinners at the laſt Judgment, doth much differ from that which was paſſed on the firſt Sin, or which is due according to the Law of Works alone. For,

1. As to the Penalty, called the Pain of Loſs, the firſt Judgment did deprive Man of the Favour of his Creator, but the ſecond will deprive him of the Favour both of the Creator and Redeemer: the firſt Judgment deprived him of the Benefits of Innocency; the ſecond deprives him of the Benefits of Redemption, the loſs of his hopes and poſſibility of Pardon, of the Spirit, of Juſtification and Adoption, and of the Benefits which conditionally were promiſed and offered him; theſe are the Puniſhments of the laſt Judgment, which the Law of Works did never threaten to the firſt Man, or to any, as it ſtood alone.

Alſo the loſs of Glory as recovered, is the proper Penalty of the violated Law of Grace, which is more than the firſt loſs. As if a Man ſhould loſe his Purſe the ſecond time, when another hath once found it for him; or rather as if a Traitor redeemed by another, and having his Life and Honours offered him, if he will thankfully accept it and come in, ſhould by his Refuſal and Obſtinacy, loſe this recovered Life, which is offered him; which is an Addition to his former Penalty.

Beſides that the higher Degree of Glory will be loſt which Chriſt would beſtow on him, more than was loſt at firſt. The very Work of the Saints in Heaven, will to praiſe and glorify him that redeemed them, and the Father in him; which would not have been the Work of Man, if he had been innocent.

2. As to the Pain of Senſe, the laſt Judgment by the Redeemer will ſentence them to a far ſorer Puniſhment than would have befaln them, if no Saviour had been offered them, *Heb.* 10. 29. The Conſcience of *Adam* if he had not been redeemed, would never have tormented him for rejecting a Redeemer, nor for re-

fuſing

fusing or abusing his gracious Offers, and his Mercies; nor for the forfeiting of a recovered Happiness; nor for refusing of the easy Terms of the Gospel, which would have given him Christ and Salvation for the accepting; nor for neglecting any Means that tended to Recovery: no nor for refusing Repentance unto Life, nor for disobeying a Redeemer that bought him by his Blood. As all these are the Penalties of the Redeemer's Law and Judgment, so is it a sorer Penalty than Conscience would have inflicted meerly for not being perfectly innocent: and they will be far soarer Gripings and Gnawings of the never-dying Worm for the abuse of these Talents, than if we had been never trusted with any after our first Forfeiture. Yea and God himself will accordingly proportion his Punishments. So that you see that privatively and positively, or as to their Loss and their Feeling, the Redeemer will pass on them a heavier Doom than the Creator did, or would have done according to the first Law to perfect Man.

3. Another Property of the Judgment of Christ is, that *it will be final, peremptory, and excluding all farther Hopes or Possibilities of a Remedy.* So was not the first Judgment of the Creator upon faln Man. Though the Law of pure Nature knew no Remedy, nor gave Man any Hope of a Redeemer, yet did it not *exclude* a Remedy, nor put in any Bar against one; but God was free to recover his Creature if he pleased. But in the Law of Grace he hath resolved, that there shall be no more Sacrifice for Sin, but a fearful looking for of Judgment and Fire which shall devour the Adversary, *Heb.* 10. 26, 27. and that the Fire shall be everlasting, the Worm shall not die, and the Fire shall not be quenched, *Mat.* 25. *ult.* *Mat.* 13. 42, 50. *John* 5. 27. *Mat.* 5. 26. *Mat.* 3. 12. and *Luke* 3. 17. *Mark* 9. 43, 44, 45, 46, 48. He that now breaketh that pure Law that requireth perfect Innocency, (as we have all done) may fly to the Promise of Grace in Christ, and

appeal

appeal to the Law of Liberty or Deliverance to be judged by that. But he that falls under the Penalty of that Law which should have saved him, as all final Unbelievers and impenitent ungodly Persons do, hath no other to appeal to. Christ would have been a Sanctuary and Refuge to thee from the Law of Works, hadst thou but come in to him: But who shall be a Refuge to thee from the Wrath of Christ? The Gospel would have freed thee from the Curse of the Law of Works, if thou hadst but believed and obeyed it: But what shall free thee from the Condemnation of the Gospel? Had there no Accusation lain against thee, but that thou wast in general a Sinner; that is, that thou wast not perfectly innocent, Christ would have answered that Charge by his Blood. But seeing thou art also guilty of those special Sins which he never shed his Blood for, who shall deliver thee from that Accusation? When Christ gave himself a Ransom for Sinners, it was with this Resolution both in the Father and himself, that none should ever be pardoned, justified or saved by that Ransom, that did not in the time of this Life sincerely return to God by Faith in the Redeemer, and live in sincere obedience to him, and persevering herein. So that he plainly *excepted* final Infidelity, Impenitency and Rebellion from Pardon: He never died for the final Non-performance of the Conditions of the New Covenant. So that his Judgment for these will be peremptory and remediless. If you say, Why cannot God find out a Remedy for this Sin, as well as he did for the first? I say, God cannot lie, *Tit.* 1. 2. He must be true and faithful, as necessarily as he must be God, because of the absolute Perfection of his Nature; and he hath said and resolved, that there shall be no more Remedy.

Many other Properties of God's Judgment general there are, as that Righteousness, Impartiality, Inflexibility, and the like, which because I would not make my Discourse too long, I will pass over, contenting my self

ſelf with the mention of theſe which are proper to the Judgment of the Redeemer according to his own Laws in ſpecial.

XII. The twelfth and laſt thing which I promiſed to unfold, is, *The Execution of this Judgment:* Here I ſhould ſhew you both the Certainty of the Execution, and by whom it will be, and how: but having done all this already in the third Part of the foreſaid *Book of Reſt*, I ſhall now only give this brief Touch of it.

No ſooner is the dreadful Sentence paſt, *Go ye curſed into everlaſting Fire*, but away they muſt be gone: There is no delay, much leſs any Reprieve to be expected; and yet much leſs is there any hope of an Eſcape. If the Judg once ſay, *Take him Jailor*; and if Chriſt ſay, *Take him Devils, you that ruled and deceived him, now torment him:* all the World cannot reſcue one ſuch Soul. It will be in vain to look about for help. Alas, there is none but Chriſt can help you; and he will not, becauſe you refuſed his help: Nay, we may ſay, *He cannot*; not for want of Power, but becauſe he is True and Juſt, and therefore will make good that Word which you believed not. It is in vain then to cry to Hills to fall on you, and the Mountains to cover you from the Preſence of him that ſitteth on the Throne. It will be in vain now to repent, and wiſh you had not ſlighted your Salvation, nor ſold it for a little Pleaſure to your Fleſh. It will be then in vain to cry, *Lord, Lord, open to us; O ſpare us; O pity us; O do not caſt us into theſe hideous Flames! Do not turn us among Devils! Do not torment thy redeemed ones in this Fire!* All this will be then too late.

Poor Sinner, whoever thou art that readeſt or heareſt theſe Lines, I beſeech thee in Compaſſion to thy Soul, conſider how fearful the Caſe of that Man will be, that is newly doomed to the *Everlaſting Fire*, and is haled to the Execution without Remedy! And what

mad

mad Men are those that now do no more to prevent such a Misery, when they might do it on such easy Terms, and now have so fair an Opportunity in their hands.

The time was when Repentance might have done thee good: but *then* all thy Repentings be in vain. *Now* while the Day of thy Visitation lasteth, hadst thou but a Heart to pray and cry for Mercy, in Faith and Fervency through Christ, thou mightest be heard. But then Praying and Crying will do no good, shouldst thou roar out in the Extremity of thy Horror and Amazement, and beseech the Lord Jesus but to forgive thee one Sin, or to send thee on Earth once more, and to try thee once again in the Flesh, whether thou wouldst not love him, and lead a holy Life, it would be all in vain. Nay, shouldst thou beg but one Hour before you were cast into those Flames, it would not be heard; it would do thee no good. How earnestly did a deceased Gentleman, *Luke* 16. 24. beg of *Abraham* for one Drop of Water from the Tip of *Lazarus*'s Finger to cool his Tongue, because he was tormented in the Flame: And what the better was he? He was sent to remember that he had his good things in this Life; and that *Remembrance* would torment him more. And do not wonder or think much at this, that Christ will not then be entreated by the Ungodly. You shall then have a *Remember* too from Christ or Conscience. He may soon stop thy Mouth, and leave thee speechless, and say, *Remember Man, that I did one Day send thee a Message of Peace, and thou wouldst not hear it. I once did stoop to beseech thee to return, and thou wouldst not hear. I besought thee by the tender Mercies of God; I besought thee by all the Love that I had shewed these, by my holy Life, by my cursed Death, by the Riches of my Grace, by the Offers of my Glory; and I could not get thee to forsake the World, to deny the Flesh, to leave one beloved Sin for all this. I besought thee over and over again: I sent many a Minister to thee in my Name: I waited on thee many a Day, and Year, and all would not do: thou wouldst not consider, return and live: and now it is too late, thy Sentence is past, and cannot be recalled: away from me thou Worker of Iniquity*, Mat. 7. 22, 23.

Ah Sirs, what a Case then is the poor desperate Sinner left in! How can I write this, or how can you that read or hear it, without trembling, once think of the Condition that such forlorn Wretches will be in! When they look above them, and see the God that hath forsaken them, because they forsook him first; when they look about them, and see the Saints on one hand whom they despised, now sentenced unto Glory; and the Wicked on the other hand whom they accompanied and imitated, now judged with them to everlasting Misery: when they look below them, and see the Flames that they must abide in, even for evermore: and when the Devils begin to hale them to the Execution: O poor Souls! Now what would they give for a Christ, for a Promise, for a time of Repentance, for a Sermon of Mercy, which once they slept under, or made no account of! How is the Case altered now with them! Who would think that these are the same Men that made light of all this on Earth, that so stoutly scorned the Reproofs of the Word, that would be worldly, and fleshly, and drunk, and proud, let Preachers say what they would; and perhaps hated those that did give them warning. Now they are of another Mind; but all too late. O were there any Place for Resistance, how would they draw back, and lay hold of any thing, before they would be dragged away into those Flames! But there is no resisting; Satan's Temptations might have been resisted, but his Executions cannot: God's Judgments might have been prevented by Faith and Prayer, Repentance and a holy Life; but they cannot be resisted when they are not prevented. Glad would the miserable Sinner be, if he might but turn to *nothing*, and cease to *be*; or that he might be any thing rather than a reasonable Creature: but these Wishes are all in vain. *There is one Time, and one Way of*

Sinne

Sinner's Deliverance; *if he fail in that one, he perisheth for ever*: all the World cannot help him after that. 2 Cor. 6. 2. *I have heard thee in a time accepted: and in the Day of Salvation have I succoured thee: Behold now is the accepted Time; behold now is the Day of Salvation.* Now he saith, *Rev.* 3. 20. *Behold, I stand at the Door and knock; if any Man hear my Voice and open the door, I will come in to him, and will sup with him, and he with me.* But for the time to come hereafter, hear what he saith, *Prov.* 1. 24, 25, 26. *Because I have called, and ye refused, I have stretched out my hand, and no Man regarded; but ye have set at nought all my Counsels, and would none of my Reproof: I also will laugh at your Calamity; I will mock when your fear cometh; when your fear cometh as a Desolation, and your Destruction cometh as a Whirlwind; when Distress and Anguish cometh upon you: then shall they call upon me, but I will not answer; they shall seek me early, but they shall not find me: for that they hated Knowledg, and did not choose the Fear of the Lord; they would none of my Counsels: they despised all my Reproofs; therefore shall they eat of the Fruit of their own way, and be filled with their own Devices: for the turning away of the Simple shall slay them, and the Prosperity of Fools shall destroy them; but whoso hearkneth to me shall dwell safely, and shall be quiet from fear of Evil.* I have recited all these Words that you may see and consider, whether I have spoke any other thing than God himself hath plainly told you of.

Having said this much of the *Certainty* of the Execution, I should next have spoke somewhat of the Manner and the Instruments, and have shewed how God will be for ever the principal Cause, and Satan and their own Consciences the Instruments in part; and in what manner Conscience will do its part, and how impossible it will be to quiet or resist it. But having spoke so much of all this already elsewhere, as is said before, I will forbear here to repeat it, leaving the Reader that desireth it, there to peruse it.

The

The Uses.

Use 1. Beloved Hearers, it was not to fill your Fancies with News that God sent me hither this Day: nor to tell you of Matters that nothing concern you: nor by some terrible Words to bring you to an Hour's Amazement and no more: But it is to tell you of things that your Eyes shall see, and to foretel you of your Danger while it may be prevented, that your precious Souls may be saved at the last, and you may stand before God with Comfort at that Day. But because this will not be every Man's Case, no nor the Case of most, I must in the Name of Christ desire you to make this Day an Enquiry into your own Souls, and as in the Presence of God let your Hearts make answer to these few Questions which I shall propound and debate with you.

Qu. 1. *Do you soundly believe this Doctrine which I have preached to you?* What say you Sirs? Do you verily *believe* it as a most certain Truth, that you and I, and all the World must stand at God's Bar and be judged to everlasting Joy or Torment? I hope you do all *in some sort* believe this: but blame me not if I be jealous whether you *soundly* believe it, while we see in the World so little of the Effect of such a Belief. I confess I am forced to think that there is more Infidelity than Faith among us, when I see more Ungodliness than Godliness among us: And I can hardly believe *that* Man that will say or swear that he believeth these things, and yet liveth as carelesly and carnally as an Infidel. I know that no Man can love to be damned; yea, I know that every Man that hath a reasonable Soul, hath naturally some love to himself, and a fear of a Danger which he verily apprehendeth: he therefore that liveth without all fear, I must think liveth without all apprehension of his Danger. Custom hath taught Men to hold greater Matters to mind; that never once trembled at the Thoughts of this great Day, nor once asked his own Soul in good Sadness, *My Soul, How dost thou think then to escape?* I say, doth this Man believe that he is going to this Judgment? Well Sirs, whether you believe it or not, you will find it true: and believe it you must before you can be safe. For if you do not believe it, you will never make ready. Let me therefore perswade you in the Fear of God to consider, that it is a Matter of undoubted Truth.

1. Consider that it is the express Word of the God of Truth, revealed in Scripture as plainly as you can desire. So that you cannot be unbelieving without denying God's Word, or giving him the Lie, *Mat.* 13. 38, 39, 40, 41, 42, 43, 49, 50. *Mat.* 25. throughout, *Rom.* 2. 5, 6, 7, 9, 10, 16. and 1. 32. *John* 5. 28, 29. *The Hour is coming in which all that are in the Graves shall hear his Voice, and shall come forth: they that have done good, unto the Resurrection of Life; and they that have done evil, unto the Resurrection of Damnation.* Heb. 9. 27. *It is appointed to all Men once to die, and after this the Judgment.* Rom. 14. 9, 12. *So then every one of us shall give account of himself to God.* Rev. 20. 12. *And I saw the dead, small and great stand before God: and the Books were opened: and another Book was opened, which is the Book of Life; and the Dead were judged out of those things which were written in the Books according to their Works.* Mat. 12. 36, 37. *But I say unto you that every idle Word that Men shall speak, they shall give account thereof at the Day of Judgment: For by thy Words thou shalt be justified, and by thy Words thou shalt be condemned.* Many more most express Texts of Scripture do put the Truth of this Judgment out of all question to all that believe the Scripture, and will

ath so positively affirmed? I hope you dare

er, it is a Master-part of your Faith, if istians, and a fundamental Article of your Christ shall come again to judg the quick . So that you must believe it or renounce anity, and then you renounce Christ and :s of Mercy that you have in him. It's at you should soundly believe in Christ, and iis Judgment and Life everlasting: because bring Life and Immortality to Light in the im. 1. 10. so it was the End of his Incarth and Resurrection, to bring you thither; of his Honour and Office which he purhis Blood, to be the Lord and Judg of all *Rom.* 14. 9. *Joh.* 5. 22. If therefore you heartily this Judgment, deal plainly and say you are Infidels, and cast away the hyzor of Christianity, and let us know you, as you are.

er that it is a Truth that is known by the f Nature, that there shall be a Happiness teous, and a Misery for the Wicked after iich is evident,

we have undeniable natural Reason for it. the Righteous Governour of the World, e must make a difference among his Subling to the Nature of their Ways: which lone here, where the Wicked prosper, and afflicted; therefore it must be hereafter. there is a Necessity that God should make l Threatnings of everlasting Happiness or he right Governing of the World: for we certainly perceive that no lower things will keep Men from destroying all humane Society, and living worse than brute Beasts; and if there be a Necessity of making such Threats and Promises, then there is certainly a Necessity of fulfilling them. For God needeth no Lie or Means of deceiving, to rule the World.

2. And as we see it by Reason, so by certain Experience, that this is discernable by the Light of Nature; for all the World, or almost all do believe it. Even those Nations where the Gospel never came, and have nothing but what they have by Nature, even the most barbarous Indians acknowledg some Life after this, and a Difference of Men according as they are here; therefore you must believe thus much, or renounce your common Reason and Humanity, as well as your Christianity. Let me therefore perswade you all in the Fear of God to confirm your Souls in the Belief of this, as if you had heard Christ or an Angel from Heaven say to you, *O Man, thou art hasting to Judgment.*

Qu. 2. My next Question is, *Whether you do ever soberly consider of this great Day?* Sirs, do you use when you are alone to think with your selves, how certain and how dreadful it will be, how fast it is coming on, and what you shall do, and what Answer you mean to make at that Day? Are your Minds taken up with these Considerations? Tell me, is it so or not?

Alas Sirs! Is this a Matter to be forgotten? Is not that Man even worse than mad, that is going to God's Judgment, and never thinks of it? when if they were to be tried for their Lives at the next Assize, they would think of it, and think again, and cast 100 times which way to escape. Methinks you should rather forget to go to Bed at Night, or to eat your Meat, or do your Work, than forget so great a Matter as this.

Truly I have often in my serious Thoughts been ready to wonder that Men can think of almost any thing else, when they have so great a thing to think of. What, forget that which you must remember for ever! forget that which should force Remembrance, yea and doth force it with some, whether they will or not! A poor despairing Soul cannot forget it: He thinks which way ever he goes he is ready to be judged. O therefore Beloved, fix these Thoughts as deep in your Hearts as Thoughts can go. O be like that holy Man, that thought which way ever he went, he heard the Trumpet sound, and the Voice of the Angel calling to the World, *Arise ye Dead, and come to Judgment.* You have warning of it from God and Man, to cause you to remember it; do not then forget it. It will be a cold Excuse another Day, *Lord, I forgat this Day, or else I might have been ready:* you dare not sure trust to such Excuses.

Qu. 3. My next Question to you is, *How are you affected with the Consideration of this Day?* Barely to think of it will not serve: to think of such a Day as this with a dull and senseless Heart, is a Sign of fearful Stupidity. Did the Knees of King *Belshazzar* knock together with trembling, when he saw the Hand-writing on the Wall? *Dan.* 5. 6. How then should thy Heart be affected that seeth the Hand-writing of God as a Summons to his Bar?

When I began to preach of these things long ago, I confess the Matters seemed to me so terrible, that I was afraid that People would have run out of their Wits with Fear; but a little Experience shewed me, that many are like a Dog that is bred up in a Forge or Furnace, that being used to it, can sleep though the Hammers are beating, and the Fire and hot Iron flaming about him, when another that had never seen it, would be amazed at the sight. When Men have heard us 7 Years together, yea 20 Years, to talk of a Day of Judgment, and they *see* it not, nor *feel* any hurt, they think it is but talk, and begin to make nothing of it.

This is their Thanks to God for his Patience: Becaus his Sentence is not executed ſpeedily, therefore thei Hearts are ſet in them to do evil, *Eccleſ.* 8. 11. As i God were ſlack of his Promiſe, as ſome Men accoun Slackneſs, 2 *Pet.* 3. 9. when one Day with him is as a 1000 Years, and a 1000 Years as one Day. What i we tell you 20 Years together that you muſt die, will you not believe us, becauſe you have lived ſo long, and ſeen no Death coming?

Three or Four things there be that ſhould bring any Matter to the Heart. 1. If it be a Matter of exceeding Weight. 2. If it concern not others only, but our ſelves. 3. If it be certain. 4. If near.

All theſe things are here to be found, and therefore how ſhould your Hearts be moved at the Conſideration of this great Day!

1. What Matter can be mentioned with the Tongue of Man of greater moment? For the poor Creature to ſtand before his Maker and Redeemer, to be judged to everlaſting Joy or Torment? Alas! all the Matters of this World are Plays, and Toys, and Dreams to this; Matters of Profit or Diſprofit are nothing to it, Matters of Credit or Diſcredit are unworthy to be named with it; Matters of temporal Life or Death are nothing to it. We may ſee the poor brute Beaſts go every Day to the Slaughter, and we make no great matter of it, though their Life be as dear to them as ours to us. To be judged to an *everlaſting* Death or Torment, this is the great Danger that one would think ſhould ſhake the ſtouteſt Heart to conſider it, and awake the dulleſt Sinner to prevent it.

2. It's a Matter that concerneth every one *of your ſelves*, and every Man or Woman that ever lived upon the Earth, or ever ſhall do; I am not ſpeaking to you of the Affairs of ſome far Country that are nothing to you but only to marvel at; which you never ſaw, nor ever ſhall do: no, it is thy own ſelf, Man or Woman, that heareſt me this Day, that ſhalt as ſurely appear be-

nent-seat of Christ, as the Lord liveth, rue and faithful; and that is as sure as this Earth, or as the Heaven is over thee. heareth all this with the most careless , shall be awakened and stand with the ty; that Man that never thought of it, time in worldly Matters, shall leave all ear; that Man that will not believe these rue, but make a Jest of them, shall see t he would not believe, and *he* also shall *Godly* that waited in Hope for that Day, their full Deliverance and Coronation, there; those that have lain in the Dust ears shall rise again, and all stand there. ver thou art, believe it, thou maist better without Meat, to see without Light, to and abide for ever on Earth, than to m that Appearance. Willing or unwil- be there. And should not a Matter then neth *thy self*, go near thy Heart, and awake Security?

is a Matter of unquestionable Certainty, hewed you already, and more would do if ing to known Infidels. If the careless y just Reason to think it were uncertain, ess were more excusable. Methinks a affected with that which he is certain shall in a manner as if it were now in doing, e perfectly *know that the Day of the Lord so* ith the Apostle.

t is not only *certain*, but it is *near*; and ld affect you the more. I confess, if it far off, yet seeing it will come at last, it fully regarded: But when the Judg is at *nes* 5. 9. and we are almost at the Bar, ort a time to this Assize, what Soul that l be secure?

Alas Sirs! what is a little time when it is gone? how quickly ſhall you and I be all in another World, and our Souls receive their particular Judgment, and ſo wait till the Body be raiſed and judged to the ſame Condition? It is not 100 Years in all likelihood, till every Soul of us ſhall be in Heaven or Hell: and it's like, not half or a quarter of that time, but it will be ſo with the greater part of us; and what is a Year or two or 100? how ſpeedily is it come? how many a Soul that is now in Heaven or Hell, within 100 Years dwelt in the Places that you now dwell in, and ſat in the Seats you now *ſit* in? And now their time is paſt, what is it? Alas, how quickly will it be ſo with us! You know not when you go to Bed, but you may be judged by the next Morning; or when you riſe, but you may be judged before Night: but certainly you know that ſhortly it will be; and ſhould not this then be laid to Heart? Yea the general Judgment will not be long: For certainly we live in the End of the World.

Qu. 4. My next Queſtion is, *Whether are you ready for this dreadful Judgment when it comes, or not?* Seeing it is *your ſelves* then muſt be tried, I think it concerns you to ſee that you be prepared. How often hath Chriſt warned us in the Goſpel, that we be *always ready*, becauſe we know not the Day or Hour of his coming? *Matth.* 24. 44, 42. and 25. 13. 1 *Theſſ.* 5. 6. and told us how ſad a time it will be to thoſe that are unready, *Mat.* 25. 11, 12. Did Men but well know what a Meeting and Greeting there will be between Chriſt and an unready Soul, it would ſure ſtartle them, and make them look about them. What ſay you, beloved Hearers, are you *ready* for Judgment, or are you not? Methinks a Man that knoweth he ſhall be judged, ſhould ask himſelf the queſtion every day of his Life; am I ready to give up my Account to God? Do not you uſe to ask this of your own Hearts? unleſs you be careleſs whether you be saved or damned, methinks you should, and ask it *seriously*.

Qu. *But who be they that are ready? how shall I know whether I be ready or not?*

Answ. There is a twofold Readiness. 1. When you are in a *safe* Case. 2. When you are in a *comfortable* Case, in regard of that Day. The latter is very *desirable*, but the first is of *absolute Necessity*: this therefore is it that you must principally enquire after.

In general, all those, and only those are ready for Judgment, who shall be justified and saved, and not condemned when Judgment comes; they that have a good Cause in a Gospel-sense. It may be known before hand who these are; for Christ judgeth, as I told you, by his Law. And therefore find out whom it is that the Law of Grace doth justify or condemn, and you may certainly know whom the Judg will justify or condemn; for he judgeth righteously.

If you further ask me who these are; remember that I told you before that every Man that is personally righteous by fulfilling the Conditions of Salvation in the Gospel, shall be saved; and he that is found unrighteous, as having not fulfilled them, shall perish at that Day.

Qu. *Who are those?*

Answ. I will tell you them in a few Words, lest you should forget, because it is a Matter that your Salvation or Damnation dependeth upon.

1. The Soul that unfeignedly repenteth of his former sinful Course, and turneth from it in Heart and Life, and loveth the Way of Godliness which he hated, and hateth the Way of Sin which he loved, and is become throughly a new Creature, being born again and sanctified by the Spirit of Christ, shall be justified: but all others shall certainly be condemned.

Good News to repenting converted Sinners: but sad to impenitent, and him that knows not what this means.

2. That

2. That Soul that feeling his Misery under Sin, and the Power of Satan, and the Wrath of God, doth believe what Christ hath done and suffered for Man's Restauration and Salvation, and thankfully accepteth him as his only Saviour and Lord, on the Terms that he is offered in the Gospel, and to those Ends, even to justify him, and sanctify and guide him, and bring him at last to everlasting Glory; that Soul shall be justified at Judgment: and he that doth not, shall be condemned.

Or in short, in Scripture-phrase, *He that believeth shall be saved, and he that believeth not shall be condemned*, Mar. 16. 16.

3. The Soul that hath had so much Knowledg of the Goodness of God, and his Love to Man in Creation, Redemption, and the following Mercies, and hath had so much Conviction of the Vanity of all Creatures, as thereupon to love God more than *all* things below, so that *he* hath the chiefest room in the Heart, and is preferred before all Creatures ordinarily in a time of trial; that Soul shall be justified at Judgment, and all others shall be condemned.

4. That Soul that is so apprehensive of the absolute Soveraignty of God as Creator and Redeemer, and of the Righteousness of his Law and the Goodness of his holy Way, as that he is firmly resolved to obey him before all others, and doth accordingly give up himself to study his Will, of purpose that he may obey it, and doth walk in these holy Ways, and hath so far mortified the Flesh, and subdued the World and the Devil, that the Authority and Word of God can do more with him than any other; and doth ordinarily prevail against all the Perswasion and Interest of the Flesh, so that the main Scope and Bent of the Heart and Life is still for God; and when he sinneth he riseth again by true Repentance; I say, that Soul, and that only, shall be justified in Judgment, and be saved.

5. That

5. That Soul that hath such believing Thoughts of he Life to come, that he taketh the promised Blessed-ness for his Portion, and is resolved to venture all else upon it, and in hope of this Glory, doth set light comparatively by all things in this World, and waiteth for it as the End of this Life, choosing any suffering that God shall call him to, rather than to lose his hopes of that Felicity, and thus persevereth to the End: I say, that Soul, and none but that, shall be justified in Judg-and escape Damnation.

In these five Marks I have told you truly and briefly, who shall be justified and saved, and who shall be condemned at the Day of Judgment. And if you would have them all in five Words, they are but the Description of these five Graces, Repentance, Faith, Love, Obedience, Hope.

But though I have laid these close together for your use, yet lest you should think that in so weighty a Case I am too short in the Proof of what I so determine of, I will tell you in the express Words of many Scripture Texts, who shall be justified, and who shall be condemned.

[*John* 3. 3. Except a Man be born again, he cannot enter into the Kingdom of God. *Heb.* 12. 14. Without Holiness none shall see God. *Luke* 13. 3, 5. Except ye repent, ye shall all likewise perish. *Acts* 26. 18. I send thee to open their Eyes, and turn them from Darkness to Light, and from the Power of Satan unto God, that they may receive forgiveness of Sins, and an Inheritance among the sanctified by Faith that is in me. *John* 3. 15, 16, 17, 18, 19. Whoever believeth in him shall not perish, but have everlasting Life: he that believeth on him, is not condemned; he that believeth not, is condemned already, because he hath not believed in the Name of the only begotten Son of God; and this is the Condemnation, that Light is come into the World, and Men loved Darkness rather than Light, because their deeds were evil. *John* 5. 28, 29. The Ho is coming, in which all that are in the Graves ſhall hear his Voice, and ſhall come forth; they that have done good to the Reſurrection of Life, and they that have done evil to the Reſurrection of Damnation. *Mat.* 25. 30. Caſt the unprofitable Servant into outer Darkneſs, there ſhall be weeping and gnaſhing of Teeth. *Luke* 19. 27. But thoſe mine Enemies which would not that I ſhould reign over them, bring hither and ſlay them before me. *Mat.* 22. 12, 13. Friend, how cameſt thou in hither, not having on a Wedding-Garment? And he was ſpeechleſs. Then ſaid the King to the Servants, bind him Hand and Foot, and take him away, and caſt him into outer Darkneſs, *&c. Mat.* 5. 20. For I ſay unto you, that except your Righteouſneſs exceed the Righteouſneſs of the Scribes and Phariſees, ye ſhall in no wiſe enter into the Kingdom of Heaven. *Mat.* 7. 21. Not every one that ſaith, Lord, Lord, ſhall enter into the Kingdom of Heaven; but he that doth the Will of my Father which is in Heaven. *Heb.* 5. 6. He is become the Author of eternal Salvation to all them that obey him. *Rev.* 22. 14. Bleſſed are they that do his Commandments, that they may have right to the Tree of Life, and may enter in by the Gate into the City. *Rom.* 8. 1, 13. There is then no Condemnation to them that are in Chriſt Jeſus, that walk not after the Fleſh, but after the Spirit. For if ye live after the Fleſh, ye ſhall die: but if ye through the Spirit do mortify the Deeds of the Body, ye ſhall live. *Rom.* 8. 9. If any Man have not the Spirit of Chriſt, he is none of his. *Gal.* 5. 18. But if ye be led of the Spirit, ye are not under the Law. *Gal.* 6. 7, 8. Be not deceived, God is not mocked: for whatſoever a Man ſoweth, that ſhall he alſo reap: for he that ſoweth to the Fleſh, ſhall of the Fleſh reap Corruption; but he that ſoweth to the Spirit, ſhall of the Spirit reap Life Everlaſting. *Mat.* 6. 21. For where your Treaſure is, there will your Heart be alſo.] Read *Pſal.* 1. and many other Texts to this purpoſe, of which ſome are

iave told you from God's Word, how you
ether you are ready for Judgment, which
hing that I would advise you to enquire

it shift do you make to keep your Souls
l Terrors, as long as you remain unready
? How do you keep the Thoughts of
ur Mind, that they do not break your
eet you in your Business, and haunt you
u go, while Judgment is so near, and
nready? But I shall proceed to my next

l in the last place, to those of you that are
, nor in a Condition wherein you may
t Day; my Question is, *How are you re-
for Judgment for the time to come?* Will you
han you have done hitherto? Or will you
selves with all your Might, to prepare for
? methinks you should be now past all
ays, or farther Doubtings about such a
l by the Consideration of what I have said
should be fully resolved to lose no more
esently awake, and set upon the Work.
should all say, We will do any thing that
ll direct us to do, rather than we will be
is final Doom. O that there were but such
, that you were truly *willing* to follow the
dance of the Lord, and to use but those
isonable Means which he hath prescribed
ord, that you may be ready for that Day!
hard matter for me to tell you, or my self,
t we must do if we will be happy; and it
ard matter to *do* it so far as we are truly
the Difficulty is to be *truly* and *throughly*
is Work. If I shall tell you what you

must do for Preparation, shall I not lose my Labour? Will you resolve and promise in the Strength of Grace, that you will faithfully and speedily endeavour to practise it, whoever shall gainsay it? Upon hope of this, I will set you down some brief Directions, which you must follow, if ever you will with Comfort look the Lord Jesus in the Face at the Hour of Death, or in the Day of Judgment.

The first Direction is this, *See that your Souls be sincerely established in the Belief of this Judgment and everlasting Life:* For if you do not soundly believe it, you will not seriously prepare for it. If you have the Judgment and Belief of an Infidel, you cannot have the Heart or the Life of a Christian. Unbelief shuts out the most of the World from Heaven: see that it do not so by you. If you say you cannot believe what you would: I answer, Feed not your Unbelief by Wilfulness or Unreasonableness; use God's Means to overcome it, and shut not your Eyes against the Light, and then try the Issue, *Heb.* 3. 12, 13, 15, 16, 17, 18, 19.

The second Direction. *Labour diligently to have a sound Understanding of the Nature of the Laws and Judgment of God.* On what Terms it is that he dealeth with Mankind: and on what Terms he will judg them to Life or Death: and what the Reward and Punishment is. For if you know not the Law by which you must be judged, you cannot know how to prepare for the Judgment. Study the Scripture therefore, and mark who they be that God promiseth to save, and who they be that he threatneth to condemn. For according to that Word will the Judgment pass.

The third Direction. *See that you take it as the very Business of your Lives, to make ready for that Day.* Understand that you have no other Business in this World, but what doth necessarily depend on this. What else have

have you to do, but to provide for everlasting, and to use Means to sustain your own Bodies and others, of purpose for this Work, till it be happily done? Live therefore as Men that make this the main Scope and Care of their Lives; and let all things else come in but on the by. Remember every Morning when you awake, that you must spend that Day in Preparation for your Account, and that God doth give it you for that end. When you go to Bed, examine your Hearts, what you have done that Day in the Preparation for your last Day: And take that time as lost which doth nothing to this end.

The fourth Direction. *Use frequently to think of the Certainty, Nearness and Dreadfulness of that Day, to keep Life in your Affections and Endeavours, lest by Inconsiderateness your Souls grow stupid and negligent.* Otherwise, because it is out of sight, the Heart will be apt to grow hardned and secure. And do not think of it slightly, as a common thing, but purposely set your selves to think of it, that it may rouze you up to such Affections and Endeavours as in some measure are answerable to the Nature of the thing.

The fifth Direction. *Labour to have a lively Feeling on thy Heart, of the Evil and Weight of that Sin which thou art guilty of, and of the Misery into which it hath brought thee, and would further bring thee if thou be not delivered, and so to feel the Need of a Deliverer.* This must prepare thee to partake of Christ now; and if thou partake not of him now, thou canst not be saved by him then. It is these Souls that now make *light* of their Sin and Misery, that must then feel them so *heavy*, as to be pressed by them into the infernal Flames. And those that *now* feel little need of a Saviour, they shall *then* have none to save them, when they feel their Need.

The sixth Direction. *Understand and believe the sufficiency of that Ransom and Satisfaction to Justice, which Christ hath made for thy Sins and for the World, and how freely and universally it is offered in the Gospel.* Thy Sin is not uncurable or unpardonable, nor thy Misery remediless; God hath provided a Remedy in his Son Christ, and brought it so near thy Hands, that nothing but thy neglecting, or wilful refusing it, can deprive thee of the Benefit. Settle thy Soul in this Belief.

The seventh Direction. *Understand and believe, that for all Christ's Satisfaction, there is an absolute Necessity of sound Faith and Repentance to be in thy own self, before thou canst be a Member of him, or be pardoned, adopted or justified by his Blood.* He died not for final Infidelity and Impenitency, as predominant in any Soul. As the Law of his Father which occasioned his Suffering, required perfect Obedience or Suffering: So his own Law, which he hath made for the Conveyance of his Benefits, doth require yet true Faith and Repentance of Men themselves, before they shall be pardoned by him; and sincere Obedience and Perseverance, before they shall be glorified.

The eighth Direction. *Rest not therefore in an unrenewed, unsanctified State; that is, till this Faith and Repentance be wrought on thy own Soul, and thou be truly broken off from thy former sinful Course, and from all things in this World; and art dedicated, devoted and resigned unto God.* Seeing this Change *must* be made, and these Graces *must* be had, or thou must certainly perish: in the Fear of God, see that thou give no ease to thy Mind till thou art thus changed. Be content with nothing till this be done. Delay not another Day. How canst thou live merrily, or sleep quietly in such a Condition, as if thou shouldst die in it, thou shouldst perish for ever? Especially when thou art every Hour uncertain whether thou shalt see another Hour, and not be presently snatch'd away by Death. Methinks while thou art in so sad a Case, which way ever thou art going, or whatever thou art doing, it should still come into thy Thoughts, *O what if I should die before I be regenerate, and have part in Christ!*

The ninth Direction. *Let it be the daily Care of thy Soul, to mortify thy fleshly Desires, and overcome this World; and live as in a continual Conflict with Satan, which will not be ended till thy Life do end.* If any thing destroy thee by drawing away thy Heart from God, it will be thy carnal Self, thy fleshly Desires, and the Allurements of this World, which is the Matter that they feed upon. This therefore must be the earnest Work of thy Life to subdue this Flesh, and set light by this World, and resist the Devil, that by these would destroy thee. It is the common Case of miserable Hypocrites, that at first they list themselves under Christ as for a Fight, but they presently forget their State and Work; and when they are once in their own Conceit regenerate, they think themselves so safe, that there is no farther Danger; and thereupon they do lay down their Arms, and take that which they miscall their Christian Liberty, and indulge and please that Flesh whch they promised to mortify, and close with the World which they promised to contemn, and so give up themselves to the Devil, whom they promised to fight against. If once you apprehend that all your Religion lieth in meer Believing, that all shall go well with you, and that the Bitterness of Death is past, and in a forbearance of some disgraceful Sins, and being much in the Exercise of your Gifts, and in external Ways of Duty, and giving God a cheap and plausible Obedience in those things only which the Flesh can spare; you are then faln into that deceitful Hypocrisy, which will as surely condemn you, as open Profaneness, if you get not out of it. You must live as in a Fight, or you cannot overcome. You *must* live loose from all things in *this World*, if you will be ready for *another*. You *must* not live after the Flesh, but mortify it by the Spirit, if you would not die, but live for ever, *Rom.* 8. 13. These things are not indifferent, but of flat Necessity.

The tenth Direction. *Do all your Works as Men that must be judged for them.* It is not enough (at least in point of Duty and Comfort) that you judg this Preparation in general to be the main Business of your Lives, but you should also order your *particular Actions* by these Thoughts, and measure them by their *Respects* to this approaching Day. Before you venture on them, enquire whether they will bear weight in Judgment, and be sweet or bitter when they are brought to Trial; both for Matter and Manner, this must be observed. O that you would remember this when Temptations are upon you, when you are tempted to give up your Minds to the World, and drown your selves in earthly Cares: Will you bethink you soberly whether you would hear of this at Judgment, and whether the World will be then as sweet as now, and whether this be the best Preparation for your Trial? When you are tempted to be drunk, or to spend your precious time in Ale-houses, or vain unprofitable Company, or at Cards or Dice, or any sinful or needless Sports; bethink you then, whether this will be comfortable at the reckoning? and whether time be no more worth to one that is so near Eternity, and must make so strict an Account of his Hours? and whether there be not many better Works before you, in which you might spend your time to your greater Advantage, and to your greater Comfort when it comes to a review? When you are tempted to Wantonness, Fornication, or any other fleshly Intemperance, bethink you soberly, with what Face these Actions will appear at Judgment, and whether they will be *then* pleasant or displeasant to you. So

when

when you are tempted to neglect the daily Worſhipping of God in your Families, and the catechiſing and teaching of your Children or Servants, eſpecially on the Lord's Day, bethink your ſelves then, what account you will give of this to Chriſt, when he that entruſted you with the Care of your Children and Servants, ſhall call you to a reckoning for the Performance of that Truſt?

The like muſt be remembred in the very manner of our Duties. How diligently ſhould a Miniſter ſtudy; how earneſtly ſhould he perſwade; how unweariedly ſhould he bear all Oppoſitions and ungrateful Returns; and how carefully ſhould he watch over each particular Soul of his Charge (as far as is poſſible) when he remember that he muſt ſhortly be accountable for all in Judgment? and how importunate ſhould we all be with Sinners for their Converſion, when we conſider that we our ſelves alſo muſt ſhortly be judged? Can a Man be cold and dead in Prayer, that hath any true Apprehenſion of that Judgment upon his Mind, where he muſt be accountable for all his Prayers and Performances? O remember, and ſeriouſly remember, when you ſtand before the Miniſter to hear the Word, and when you are on your Knees to God in Prayer, in what a manner that ſame Perſon, even your ſelves, muſt ſhortly ſtand at the Bar of the dreadful God! Did theſe Thoughts get throughly to Mens Hearts, they would awaken them out of their ſleepy Devotions, and acquaint them that it is a ſerious Buſineſs to be a Chriſtian. How careful ſhould we be of our Thoughts and Words, if we believingly remembred that we muſt be accountable for them all! How carefully ſhould we conſider what we do with our Riches, and with all that God giveth us? and how much more largely ſhould we expend it for his Service in Works of Piety and Charity, if we believingly remembred that we muſt be judged according to what we have done, and give account of every Talent that we receive? Certainly the believing Conſideration of

Judgment, might make us all better Christians than we are, and keep our Lives in a more innocent and profitable Frame.

The eleventh Direction. *As you will certainly renew your Failings in this Life, so be sure that you daily renew your Repentance, and fly daily to Christ for a renewed Pardon, that no Sin may leave its sting in your Souls.* It is not your *first* Pardon that will serve the turn for your *latter* Sins. Not that you must *purpose* to *sin*, and *purpose* to *repent* when you have done, as a Remedy: for that is an hypocritical and wicked *Purpose* of Repenting, which is made a Means to maintain us in our Sins; but Sin must be avoided as far as we can; and Repentance and Faith in the Blood of Christ must remedy that which we could not avoid. The Righteousness of Pardon in Christ's Blood is useful to us only so far as we are Sinners, and cometh in where our imperfect inherent Righteousness doth come short; but must not be purposely chosen before Innocency: I mean, we must rather choose as far as we can, to obey and be innocent, than to sin and be pardoned, if we were sure of Pardon.

The twelfth Direction. In this vigilant, obedient, penitent Course, with Confidence upon God as a Father, rest upon the Promise of Acceptance and Remission, through the Merits and Intercession of him that redeemed you: Look up in hope to the Glory that is before you, and believe that God will make good his Word, and the patient Expectation of the Righteous shall not be in vain. Chearfully hold on in the Work that you have begun: and as you serve a better Master than you did before your Change, so serve him with more Willingness, Gladness and Delight. Do not entertain hard Thoughts of him, or of his Service, but rejoice in your unspeakable Happiness of being admitted into his Family and Favour through Christ. Do not serve him in drooping Dejection and Discouragement, but with Love, and Joy, and filial Fear. Keep in the Communion of his Saints, where he is chearfully and faithfully praised and honoured, and where is the greatest visible Similitude of Heaven upon Earth; especially in the Celebration of the Sacrament of Christ's Supper, where he seals up a renewed Pardon in his Blood, and where unanimously we keep the Remembrance of his Death until he come. Do not cast your selves out of the Communion of the Saints, from whom to be cast out by just Censure and Exclusion, is a dreadful Emblem and Fore-runner of the Judgment to come, where the Ungodly shall be cast out of the Presence of Christ and his Saints for ever.

I have now finished the Directions, which I tender to you for your Preparation for the Day of the Lord; and withal my whole Discourse on this weighty Point. What Effect all this shall have upon your Hearts, the Lord knows; it is not in my Power to determine. If you are so far blinded and hardned by Sin and Satan, as to make light of all this, or coldly to commend the Doctrine, while you go on to the End in your carnal worldly Condition as before; I can say no more, but tell thee again that Judgment is near, when thou wilt bitterly bewail all this too late. And among all the rest of the Evidence that comes in against thee, this Book will be one which shall testify to thy Face before Angels and Men, that thou wast told of that Day, and intreated to prepare.

But if the Lord shall shew thee so much Mercy as to open thy Eyes, and break in upon thy Heart, and by sober Consideration turn it to himself, and cause thee faithfully to take the Warning that hath been give thee, and to obey these Directions, I dare assure thee from the Word of the Lord, that this Judgment which will be so dreadful to the Ungodly, and the Beginning of their endless Terrour and Misery, will be as joyful to thee, and the Beginning of thy Glory. The Saviour that thou hast believed in and sincerely obeyed, will not condemn thee, *Psal.* 1. 5, 6. *Rom.* 8. 1. *John* 3. 16. It is part of his Business to justify thee before the World, and to glorify his Merits, his Kingly Power, his Holiness, and his rewarding Justice in thy Absolution and Salvation. He will account it a righteous thing to recompense Tribulation to thy Troublers, and Rest to thy self; when the Lord Jesus shall be revealed from Heaven with his Mighty Angels, in flaming Fire, taking Vengeance on them that know not God, and that obey not the Gospel of our Lord Jesus Christ; who shall be punished with everlasting Destruction from the Presence of the Lord, and from the Glory of his Power: Even then shall he come to be glorified in his Saints, and to be admired in all them that believe in that Day; even because his Servants Testimony, and his Spirits among them was believed, 2 *Thess.* 1. 6, 7, 8, 9, 10. That Day will be the great Marriage of the Lamb, and the Reception of thee, and all the Saints into the Glory of thy Beloved, to which they had a Right at their first Consent and Contract upon Earth: And when the Bridegroom comes, thou who art ready shalt go into the Marriage, when the Door shall be shut against the sleepy negligent World; and though they *cry*, *Lord*, *Lord*, *open to us*, they shall be repulsed with a *Verily I know you not*, *Mat.* 25. 10, 11, 12, 13. For this Day which others fear, mayest thou long, and hope, and pray, and wait, and comfort thy self in all Troubles with the Remembrance of it, 1 *Cor.* 15. 55, 56, 57, 58. 1 *Thess.* 4. 17, 18. If thou wert ready to be offered to Death for Christ, or when the time of thy Departing is at hand, thou mayest look back on the good Fight which thou hast fought, and on the Course which thou hast finished, and on the Faith which thou hast kept, and mayest confidently conclude, that henceforth there is laid up for thee *a Crown of Righteousness*, which *the Lord the Righteous Judg* shall give thee at that Day; and not to thee only, but unto all them also that love his Appearing, 2 *Tim.* 4. 6, 7, 8. *Even so, come Lord Jesus*, Rev. 22. 20.

The Danger of ſlighting Chriſt and his Goſpel.

Mat. 22. 5. *But they made light of it.*

THE bleſſed Son of God, that thought not enough to die for the World, but would himſelf alſo be the Preacher of Grace and Salvation, doth comprize in this Parable the Sum of his Goſpel. By the King that is here ſaid to make the Marriage, is meant God the Father that ſent his Son into the World to cleanſe them from their Sins, and eſpouſe them to himſelf. By his Son for whom the Marriage is made, is meant the Lord Jeſus Chriſt, the eternal Son of God, who took to his God-head the Nature of Man, that he might be capable of being their Redeemer when they had loſt themſelves in Sin. By the Marriage is meant the Conjunction of Chriſt to the Soul of Sinners, when he giveth up himſelf to them to be their Saviour, and they give up themſelves to him as his redeemed Ones, to be ſaved and ruled by him; the Perfection of which Marriage will be at the Day of Judgment, when the Conjunction between the whole Church and Chriſt ſhall be ſolemnized. The Word here tranſlated *Marriage*, rather ſignifieth the *Marriage-Feaſt*; and the meaning is, that the World is invited by the Goſpel to come in and partake of Chriſt and Salvation, which comprehendeth both Pardon, Juſtification and Right to Salvation, and all other Privileges of the Members of Christ. The *Invitation* is God's Offer of Christ and Salvation in the Gospel; the Servants that invite them are the Preachers of the Gospel, who are sent forth by God to that end; the Preparation for the Feast there mentioned, is the Sacrifice of Jesus Christ, and the enacting of a Law of Grace, and opening a Way for revolting Sinners to return to God. There is a mention of sending second Messengers, because God useth not to take the first Denial, but to exercise his Patience till Sinners are obstinate. The first Persons invited are the Jews; upon their obstinate Refusal they are sentenced to Punishment; and the Gentiles are invited, and not only invited, but by powerful Preaching, and Miracles, and effectual Grace compelled, that is, infallibly prevailed with to come in. The Number of them is so great, that the House is filled with the Guests; many come sincerely, not only looking at the Pleasure of the Feast, that is, at the Pardon of Sin, and Deliverance from the Wrath of God, but also at the Honour of the Marriage, that is, of the Redeemer, and their Profession by giving up themselves to an holy Conversation: but some come in only for the Feast, that is, Justification by Christ, having not the Wedding-garment of sound Resolution for Obedience in their Life, and looking only at themselves in believing, and not to the Glory of their Redeemer: and these are sentenced to everlasting Misery, and speed as ill as those that came not in at all; seeing a Faith that will not work, is but like that of the Devil; and they that look to be pardoned and saved by it, are mistaken, as *James* sheweth, *ch.* 2. 24.

The Words of my Text contain a Narration of the ill Entertainment that the Gospel findeth with many to whom it is sent, even after a first and second Invitation. They make light of it, and are taken up with other things. Though it be the Jews that were first guilty, they have too many followers among us Gentiles to this Day.

Doct.

Doct. *For all the wonderful Love and Mercy that God hath manifested in giving his Son to be the Redeemer of the World, and which the Son hath manifested in redeeming them by his Blood; for all his full Preparation, by being a sufficient Sacrifice for the Sins of all; for all his personal Excellencies, and that full and glorious Salvation that he hath procured; and for all his free Offers of these, and frequent and earnest Invitation of Sinners: yet many do make light of all this, and prefer their worldly Enjoyments before it. The ordinary Entertainment of all is by Contempt.*

Not that all do so, or that all continue to do so who were once guilty of it: for God hath his Chosen whom he will compel to come in. But till the Spirit of Grace overpower the dead and obstinate Hearts of Men, they hear the Gospel as a common Story, and the great Matters contained in it go not to the Heart.

The Method in which I shall handle this Doctrine is this.

1. I shall shew you what it is that Men make light of.

2. What this Sin of making light of it is.

3. The Cause of the Sin.

4. The Use of the Doctrine.

I. The thing that carnal Hearers make light of, is, 1. The Doctrine of the Gospel it self, which they hear regardlesly. 2. The Benefits offered them therein: which are, 1. Christ himself. 2. The Benefits which he giveth.

Concerning Christ himself, the Gospel, 1. Declareth his Person and Nature, and the great things that he hath done and suffered for Man; his redeeming him from the Wrath of God by his Blood, and procuring a Grant of Salvation with himself. Furthermore, the same Gospel maketh an Offer of Christ to Sinners, that if they will accept him on his easy and reasonable Terms, he will be their Saviour, the Physician of their Souls, their Husband and their Head.

2. The Benefits that he offereth them, are these. 1. That with these blessed Relations to him, himself, and Interest in him, they shall have the Pardon of all their Sins past, and be saved from God's Wrath, and be set in a sure way of obtaining a Pardon for all the Sins that they shall commit hereafter, so they do but obey sincerely, and turn not again unto the Rebellion of their Unregeneracy. 2. They shall have the Spirit to become their Guide and Sanctifier, and to dwell in their Souls, and help them against their Enemies, and conform them more and more to his Image, and heal their Diseases, and bring them back to God. 3. They shall have Right to everlasting Glory when this Life is ended, and shall be raised up thereto at the last; besides many excellent Privileges in the Way, in Means, Preservation and Provision, and the Foretaste of what they shall enjoy hereafter: all these Benefits the Gospel offereth to them that will have Christ on his reasonable Terms. The Sum of all is in 1 *John* 5. 11, 12. *This is the Record that God hath given us eternal Life, and this Life is in his Son: He that hath the Son hath Life, and he that hath not the Son hath not Life.*

II. *What this Sin of making light of the Gospel is?* 1. To make light of the Gospel, is to take no great heed to what is spoken, as if it were not a certain Truth, or else were a Matter that little concerned them, or as if God had not written these things for them. 2. When the Gospel doth not *affect* Men, or go to their *Hearts*; but though they seem to attend to what is said, yet Men are not *awakened* by it from their Security, nor doth it work in any measure such holy Passion in their Souls, as Matters of such everlasting Consequence should do; this is making light of the Gospel of Salvation. When we tell Men what Christ hath done and suffered for their Souls, and it scarce moveth them: We tell them of keen and cutting Truths, but nothing will pierce them; we can make them hear, but we

cannot

cannot make them feel; our Words take up in the Porch of their Ears and Fancies, but will not enter into the inward Parts; as if we ſpake to Men that had no Hearts or Feeling; this is a making light of Chriſt and Salvation. *Acts* 28. 26, 27. Hearing ye ſhall hear, and ſhall not underſtand; ſeeing ye ſhall ſee, and ſhall not perceive: For the Heart of this People is waxen groſs, and their Ears are dull of hearing, their Eyes are cloſed, *&c.*

3. When Men have no high Eſtimation of Chriſt and Salvation, but whatſoever they may ſay with their Tongues, or dreamingly and ſpeculatively believe, yet in their ſerious and practical Thoughts, they have a higher Eſtimation of the Matters of this World, than they have of Chriſt and the Salvation that he hath purchaſed; this is a making light of him. When Men account the Doctrine of Chriſt to be but a Matter of Words and Names, as *Gallio*, *Acts* 18. 4. or as *Feſtus*, *Acts* 25. 19. a ſuperſtitious Matter about one Jeſus who was dead, and *Paul* ſaith is alive: or ask the Preachers of the Goſpel as the *Athenians*, *Acts* 17. 18. *What will this Babler ſay?* This is a Contempt of Chriſt.

4. When Men are informed of the Truths of the Goſpel, and on what Terms Chriſt and his Benefits may be had, and how it is the Will of God that they ſhould *believe* and *accept* the Offer; and that he *commandeth* them to do it upon Pain of Damnation; and yet Men *will* not conſent, unleſs they could have Chriſt on Terms of their own: they will not part with their worldly Contents, nor lay down their Pleaſures and Profits, and Honour at his Feet, as being content to take ſo much of them only as he will give them back, and as is conſiſtent with his Will and Intereſt, but think it is a hard ſaying, that they muſt forſake all in Reſolution for Chriſt; this is a making light of him and their Salvation. When Men might have part in him and all his Benefits if they *would*, and they *will* not unleſs they may keep the World too; and are reſolved to pleaſe their Fleſh,

whatever comes of it; this is a high Contempt of Christ and everlasting Life. *Mat.* 13. 21, 22. *Luke* 18. 23. you may find Examples of such as I here describe.

5. When Men will promise fair, and profess their Willingness to have Christ on his Terms, and to forsake all for him; but yet *do stick* to the World and their sinful Courses; and when it comes to *Practice*, will not be removed by all that Christ hath done and said: this is making light of Christ and Salvation. *Jer.* 42. 5. compared with 43. 2.

III. The Causes of this Sin are the next thing to be enquired after. It may seem a Wonder that ever Men that have the use of their Reason, should be so sottish as to make light of Matters of such Consequence. But the Cause is;

1. Some Men understand not the very Sense of the Words of the Gospel when they hear it, and how can they be taken with that which they understand not? Though we speak to them in plain English, and study to speak it as plain as we can; yet People have so estranged themselves from God, and the Matters of their own Happiness, that they know not what we say; as if we spoke in another Language, and as if they were under that Judgment, *Isa.* 28. 11. with stammering Lips, and with another Tongue will he speak to this People.

2. Some that do understand the *Words* that we speak, yet because they are carnal, understand not the *Matter*: for the natural Man receiveth not the things of the Spirit of God, neither can he know them, because they are spiritually discerned, 1 *Cor.* 2. 14. They are earthly, and these things are heavenly, *John* 3. 12. The things of the Spirit are not well known by bare hearsay, but by a spiritual Taste, which none have but those that are taught by the Holy Ghost, 1 *Cor.* 2.12. that we may know the things that are given us of God.

3. A

Mind apprehendeth not a *Sutableness* in
and heavenly things to his Mind, and
ts light by them, and hath no mind of
you tell him of everlasting Glory, he
if you were perswading him to go play
they are Matters of another World, and
ient; and therefore he hath no more De-
han a Fish would have to be in the fairest
han a Swine hath in a Jewel, or a Dog
iold: They may be good to others, but
ehend them as sutable to him, because
re that is otherwise inclined: he savour-
ngs of the Spirit, *Rom.* 8. 5.
n Cause of the slighting of Christ and
secret Root of *Unbelief* in Mens Hearts.
ney may pretend, they do not soundly
believe the Word of God: they are
ral to say, *the Gospel is true*; but they ne-
vidence of its Truth so far as throughly to
n of it; nor have they got their Souls
nfallibility of God's Testimony, nor con-
Truth of the particular Doctrines reveal-
oture, so far as soundly to believe them.
ut *soundly believe* the Words of this Gospel,
Sin, of the Need of Christ, and what
or you, and what you must *be* and *do* if
e saved by him, and what will become of
if you do it not; I dare say, it would
empt of Christ, and you would not make
Matters of your Salvation. But Men do
ile they say they do, and would face us
do, and verily think that they do them-
is a Root of bitterness, and an evil Heart
hat makes them depart from the living
12. and 4. 1, 2, 6. Tell any Man in this
that he shall have a Gift of 10000 pounds,
o to *London* for it; if he believe you, he
f he believe not, he will not: and if he

will not go, you may be sure he believeth not, supposing that he is able. I know a slight Belief may stand with a wicked Life: Such as Men have of the Truth of a Prognostication, *it may be true and it may be false*; but a *true and sound* Belief is not consistent with so great Neglect of the things that are believed.

5. Christ and Salvation are made light of by the World because of their desperate hardness of Heart. The Heart is hard naturally, and by Custom in sinning made more hard, especially by long abuse of Mercy, and neglect of the means of Grace, and resisting the Spirit of God. Hence it is that Men are turned into such Stones: and till God cure them of the Stone of the Heart, no wonder if they *feel* not what they know, or regard not what we say, but make light of all; 'tis hard preaching a Stone into tears, or making a Rock to tremble. You may stand over a dead Body long enough, and say to it, *O thou Carcase, when thou hast lain rotting and mouldred to Dust till the Resurrection, God will then call thee to account for thy Sin, and cast thee into everlasting Fire*, before you can make it feel what you say, or fear the Misery that is never so truly threatned. When Mens Hearts are like the High-way that is trodden to hardness by long custom in Sinning, or like the Clay that is hardned to a Stone by the heat of those Mercies that should have melted them into Repentance; when they have Consciences seared with an hot Iron, as the Apostle speaks, 2 *Tim.* 4. 2. no wonder then if they be past feeling, and working all Uncleanness with greediness, do make light of Christ and everlasting Glory. O that this were not the Case of too many of our Hearers! Had we but *living Souls* to speak to, they would hear, and feel, and not make light of what we say. I know they are naturally alive, but they are spiritually dead, as the Scripture witnesseth, *Ephes.* 2. 3. O if there were but one spark of the Life of Grace in them, the Doctrine of Salvation by Jesus Christ would appear to them to be the weightiest Business in the

ıw confident ſhould I be methinks, to pre-, and to take them off this World, and mind the Matter of another World, if I Men that had Life and Senſe and Reaſon; ſpeak to Blocks and dead Men, how ſhould ed? O how ſad a Caſe are theſe Souls llen under this fearful Judgment of ſpi-; and Deadneſs! To have a blind Mind, Heart, to be ſottiſh and ſenſleſs, *Mark* 4. 40. leſt they ſhould be converted, and uld be forgiven them.

ınd Salvation are made light of by the uſe they are wholly enſlaved to their Senſe, with lower things: the Matters of ano-e out of ſight, and ſo far from their Sen-cannot regard them; but preſent things em, in their Eyes, and in their Hands: a living Faith to prevail over Senſe, be-be ſo taken with things that are not ſeen, ıave the Word of God for their Security, nd let go things that are ſtill before their works with great Advantage, and there-h in reſiſting Faith where it is. No won-carry all before it, where there is no true ith to reſiſt, and to lead the Soul to high-s Cauſe of making light of Chriſt and Sal-reſſed here in my Text; One went to his other to his Merchandize: Men have Hou-to look after: they have Wife and Chil-they have their Body and outward Eſtate erefore they forget that they have a God, a Soul to mind; theſe Matters of the ill with them. They *ſee* theſe, but they ties: but their Souls in ſpiritual Reſpects are dead, and therefore feel not their Wants, but will let them alone in their greateſt Neceſſities; and be as quiet when they are ſtarved and languiſhing to Deſtruction, as if all were well and nothing ailed them. And hereupon poor People are wholly taken up in providing for the Body, as if they had nothing elſe to mind. They have their Trades and Callings to follow, and ſo much to do from Morning to Night, that they can find no time for Matters of Salvation. Chriſt would teach them, but they have no leiſure to hear him: the Bible is before them, but they cannot have while to read it: A Miniſter is in the Town with them, but they cannot have while to go to enquire of him what they ſhould do to be ſaved: And when they do hear, their Hearts are ſo full of the World, and carried away with theſe lower Matters, that they cannot mind the things which they hear. They are ſo full of the Thoughts and Deſires, and Cares of this World, that there is no room to pour into them the Water of Life: The Cares of the World do choak the Word, and make it become unfruitful, *Matth.* 13.22. Men cannot ſerve two Maſters, God and Mammon, but they will lean to the one, and deſpiſe the other, *Matth.* 6. 24. He that loveth the World, the Love of the Father is not in him, 1 *John* 2. 15, 16. Men cannot chooſe but ſet light by Chriſt and Salvation, while they ſet ſo much by any thing on Earth. It is that which is highly eſteemed among Men, is abominable in the Sight of God, *Luke* 16. 15. O this is the Ruine of many thouſand Souls! It would grieve the Heart of any honeſt Chriſtian, to ſee how eagerly this vain World is followed everywhere, and how little Men ſet by Chriſt, and the World to come;

r[illegible]

to compare the Care that Men have for the World, with the Care of their Souls; and the time that they lay out on the World, with that time they lay out for their Salvation: To see how the World fil's their Mouths, their Hands, their Houses, their Hearts; and Christ hath little more than a bare Title: to come into their Company, and hear no Discourse but of the World; to come into their Houses, and hear and see nothing but for the World, as if this World would last for ever, or would purchase them another. When I ask sometime the Ministers of the Gospel how their Labours succeed, they tell me, *People continue still the same, and give up themselves wholly to the World, so that they mind not what Ministers say to them, nor will give any full Entertainment to the Word, and all because of the deluding World.* And O that too many Ministers themselves did not make light of that Christ whom they preach, being drawn away with the Love of this World! In a Word, Men of a worldly Disposition do judg of things, according to worldly Advantages; therefore Christ is slighted, *Isa.* 53. 3. *He is despised and rejected of Men; they hide their faces from him, and esteem him not, as seeing no Beauty or Comeliness in him, that they should desire him.*

7. Christ and Salvation are made light of, because Men do not soberly *consider* of the Truth and Weight of these necessary things. They suffer not their Minds so long to *dwell* upon them, till they procure a due Esteem, and deeply affect their Heart; did they believe them, and not *consider* of them, how should they work? O when Men have Reason given them to think and consider of the things that most concern them, and yet they will not use it, this causeth their Contempt.

8. Christ and Salvation are made light of, because Men were never *sensible* of their *Sin and Misery*, and *extream Necessity* of Christ and his Salvation: Their Eyes were never opened to see *themselves* as they are; nor

their Hearts soundly humbled in the Sense of their Condition: if this were done, they would soon be brought to value a Saviour. A truly broken Heart can no more make light of Christ and Salvation, than a hungry Man of his Food, or a sick Man of the Means that would give him ease: but till then, our Words cannot have Access to their Hearts. While Sin and Misery is made light of, Christ and Salvation will be made light of; but when these are perceived an intolerable Burden, then nothing will serve the turn but Christ. Till Men be truly humbled, they can venture Christ and Salvation for a Lust, for a little worldly Gain, even for less than nothing: but when God hath illuminated them, and broken their Hearts, then they would give a World for a Christ; then they *must have Christ, or they die*; *all things then are Loss and Dung to them in regard of the excellent Knowledg of Christ*, Phil. 3. 8. When they are once pricked in their Hearts for Sin and Misery, then they cry out, *Men and Brethren what shall we do?* Acts 2. 37. When they are awakened by God's Judgments, as the poor Jaylor, *Acts* 16. 29. then they cry out, *Sirs, what shall I do to be saved?* This is the Reason why God will bring Men so low by Humiliation, before he bring them to Salvation.

9. Men take occasion to make light of Christ, by the *Commonness* of the Gospel; because they do hear of it every Day, the *frequency* is an Occasion to dull their Affections; I say, an Occasion, for it is no just Cause. Were it a *Rarity*, it might take more with them; but *now*, if they hear a Minister preach nothing but these saving Truths, they say, *We have these every Day*; they make not light of their Bread or Drink, their Health or Life, because they possess them *every day*; they make not light of the Sun, because it shineth *every day*; at least they should not, for the Mercy is the greater: but Christ and Salvation are made light of, because they hear of them often; *This is*, say they, *a good plain dry Sermon*: *Pearls* are trod in the dirt where they are *common*;

mon; they loath this dry Manna, *Prov.* 27. 7. The full Soul loaths the Hony-comb; but to the Hungry Soul every bitter thing is sweet.

10. Christ and Salvation are made light of, because of this disjunctive *Presumption*, either that he is sure enough *theirs already*, and God that is so merciful, and Christ that hath suffered so much for them, is surely resolved to save them, or else it may easily be obtained at any time, if it be not yet so. A conceited *Facility* to have a part in Christ and Salvation at any time, doth occasion Men to make light of them. It is true, that Grace is *free*, and the Offer is universal, according to the extent of the preaching of the Gospel; and it is true that Men may have Christ *when they will*; that is, when they are willing to have him on his Terms: but he that hath promised thee Christ, if thou be willing, hath not promised to make thee willing; and if thou art not willing *now*, how canst thou think thou shalt be willing hereafter? If thou canst make thine own Heart willing, why is it not done now? Can you do it better when Sin hath more hardned it, and God may have given thee over to thy self? O Sinners, you might do much, though you are not able of your selves to come in, if you would now subject your selves to the working of the Spirit, and set in while the Gales of Grace continue! But did you know what a hard and impossible thing it is to be so much as willing to have Christ and Grace, when the Heart is given over to it self, and the Spirit hath withdrawn its former Invitations, you would not be so confident of your own Strength to believe and repent; nor would you make light of Christ upon such foolish Confidence. If indeed it be so easy a Matter as you imagine for a Sinner to believe and repent at any time; how comes it to pass that it is done by so few, but most of the World do perish in their Impenitency, when they have all the Helps and Means that we can afford them? It is true, the thing is very reasonable and easy in it self to a pure Nature; but while Man

is blind and dead, these things are in a sort impossible to him, which are never so easy to others. It is the easiest and sweetest Life in the World to a gracious Soul to live in the Love of God, and the delightful Thoughts of the Life to come, where all their Hope and Happiness lieth: But to worldly carnal Hearts it is as easy to remove a Mountain, as to bring them to this. However, these Men are their own Condemners: for if they think it so easy a Matter to repent and believe, and so to have Christ and Right to Salvation, then have they no excuse for neglecting this which they thought so easy. O wretched impenitent Soul! what mean you to say, when God shall ask you, *Why did you not repent and love your Redeemer above the World, when you thought it so easy that you could do it at any time?*

IV. *Use* 1. We come now to the Application. And hence you may be informed of the Blindness and Folly of all carnal Men: how *contemptible* are their Judgments that think Christ and Salvation *contemptible*: and how little Reason there is why any should be moved by them, or discouraged by any of their Scorns or Contradictions.

How shall we sooner know a Man to be a Fool, than if he knows no difference between Dung and Gold? Is there such a thing as *madness* in the Word, if that Man be not mad, that sets light by Christ and his own Salvation, while he daily toils for the Dung of the Earth? And yet what pity is it to see that a Company of poor ignorant Souls will be ashamed of Godliness, if such Men as these do but deride them! Or will think hardly of a holy Life, if such as these do speak against it! Hearers, if you see any *set light* by Christ and Salvation, do you *set light* by that Man's *Wit*, and by his *Words*, and hear the Reproaches of a holy Life, as you would hear the Words of a Mad-man; not with regard, but with a Compassion of his Misery.

Use 2. What wonder if we and our preaching be despised, and the best Ministers complain of ill success, when the Ministry of the Apostles themselves did succeed no better? What wonder if for all that we can say or do, our Hearers still set light by Christ and their own Salvation, when the Apostles Hearers did the same? They that did second their Doctrines by Miracles. If any Men could have shaken and torn in pieces the Hearts of Sinners, they could have done it: If any could have laid them at their Feet, and made them all cry out as some, *What shall we do?* it would have been they. You may see then that it is not meerly for want of good Preachers that Men make light of Christ and Salvation: the first News of such a thing as the Pardon of Sin, and the Hopes of Glory, and the Danger of everlasting Misery, would turn the Hearts of Men within them, if they were as tractable in spiritual Matters as in temporal: But alas, it is far otherwise. It must not seem any strange thing, nor must it too much discourage the Preachers of the Gospel, if when they have said all that they can devise to say to win the Hearts of Men to Christ, the most do still slight him; and while they bow the Knee to him, and honour him with their Lips, do yet set so light by him in their Hearts, as to prefer every fleshly Pleasure or Commodity before him. It will be thus with many: let us be glad that it is not thus with all.

Use 3. But for closer Application. Seeing this is the great condemning Sin, before we enquire after it into the Hearts of our Hearers, it beseems us to begin at home, and see that we who are Preachers of the Gospel be not guilty of it our selves. The Lord forbid that they that have undertaken the sacred Office of revealing the Excellencies of Christ to the World, should make light of him themselves, and slight that Salvation which they do daily preach. The Lord knows we are all of us so low in our Estimation of Christ, and do this great Work so negligently, that we have cause to be ashamed of our best Sermons; but should this Sin prevail in us, we were the most miserable of all Men. Brethren, I love not Censoriousness; yet dare not befriend so vile a Sin in my self or others under pretence of avoiding it, especially when there is so great Necessity that it should be healed first in them that make it their Work to heal it in others. O that there were no cause to complain that Christ and Salvation are made light of by the Preachers of it! But, 1. Do not the negligent Studies of some speak it out? 2. Doth not their dead and drowsy Preaching declare it? Do not they make light of the Doctrine they preach, that do it as if they were half asleep, and feel not what they speak themselves?

3. Doth not the Carelesness of some Mens private Endeavours discover it? What do they for Souls? how slightly do they reprove Sin? how little do they when they are out of the Pulpit for the saving of Mens Souls?

4. Doth not the continued Neglect of those things wherein the Interest of Christ consisteth discover it? 1. The Churches Purity and Reformation; 2. Its Unity.

5. Doth not the covetous and worldly Lives of too many discover it, losing Advantages for Mens Souls for a little Gain to themselves? and most of this is because Men are Preachers before they are Christians, and tell Men of that which they never felt themselves. Of all Men on Earth, there are few that are in so sad a Condition as such Ministers: and if indeed they do believe that Scripture which they preach, methinks it should be terrible to them in their studying and preaching it.

Use 4. Beloved Hearers; the Office that God hath called us to, is, by declaring the Glory of his Grace, to help

;hrist to the saving of Mens Souls. I hope
ot that I come hither to Day on any other
ne Lord knows I had not set a Foot out of
in hope to succeed in this Work for your
ve considered and often considered, what is
hat so many thousands should perish when
one so much for their Salvation; and I find
nentioned in my Text is the Cause. It is one
iders of the World, that when God hath
World as to send his Son, aud Christ hath
sfaction by his Death sufficient for them all,
the Benefits of it so freely to them, even
ney or Price, that yet the most of the World
sh; yea the most of those that are thus
nis Word! Why here is the Reason, when
done all this, Men make light of it. God
d that *he* is not unwilling; and Christ hath
s *he* is not unwilling that Men should be re-
od's Favour and be saved; but Men are actu-
ng *themselves*. God takes not *pleasure* in the
nners, but rather that they return and live,
r. But Men take such *pleasure* in Sin, that
e before they will return. The Lord Jesus
t to be their Physician, and hath provided
cient Plaister of his own Blood: but if Men
of it, and will not apply it, what wonder
ish after all? This Scripture giveth us the
heir Perdition. This sad Experience tells
of the World is guilty of. It is a most la-
ing to see how most Men do spend their Care,
, their Pains for known Vanities, while God
are cast aside: That he who is *all*, should
m as *nothing*; and that which is *nothing*, should
m as good as *all*; that God should set Man-
n a Race where Heaven or Hell is their certain
hat they should sit down, and loiter, or run
hildish Toys of the World, and so much
Prize that they should run for. Were it but

possible for one of us to see the *whole* of this Business, as the All-seeing God doth; to see at one View both Heaven and Hell which Men are so near, and see what most Men in the World are minding, and what they are doing every Day, it would be the saddest sight that could be imagined. O how should we marvel at their Madness, and lament their Self-delusion! O poor distracted World! what is it that you run after? and what is it that you neglect? If God had never told them what they were sent into the Word to do, or whither they were going, or what was before them in another World, then they had been excusable; but he hath told them over and over, till they were weary of it. Had he left it doubtful, there had been some excuse; but it is his sealed Word, and they profess to believe it, and would take it ill of us if we should question whether they do believe it or not.

Beloved, I come not to accuse any of you particularly of this Crime: but seeing it is the commonest Cause of Mens Destruction, I suppose you will judg it the fittest Matter for our Enquiry, and deserving our greatest Care for the Cure. To which end I shall, 1. Endeavour the *Conviction* of the Guilty. 2. Shall give them such Considerations as may tend to humble and reform them. 3. I shall conclude with such Direction as may help them that are willing to escape the destroying Power of this Sin. And for the first, consider,

1. It is the Case of most Sinners to think themselves freest from those Sins that they are most enslaved to; and one reason why we cannot reform them, is, because we cannot convince them of their Guilt. It is the Nature of Sin so far to blind and befool the Sinner, that he knoweth not what he doth, but thinketh he is free from it when it reigneth in him, or when he is committing it: It bringeth Men to be so much unacquainted with themselves, that they know not what they think, or what they mean and intend, nor what they love or hate, much less what they are habituated and disposed

to. They are alive to Sin, and dead to all the Reason, Consideration and Resolution that should recover them, as if it were only by their sinning that we must know they are alive. May I hope that you that hear me to Day, are but willing to know the Truth of your Case, and then I shall be encouraged to proceed to an enquiry. God will judg impartially; why should not we do so? Let me therefore by these following Questions, try whether none of you are Slighters of Christ and your own Salvation. And follow me, I beseech you, by putting them close to your own Hearts, and faithfully answering them.

1. Things that Men highly value will be *remembred*, they will be matter of their freest and sweetest thoughts; this a known Case.

Do not those then make light of Christ and Salvation, that think of them so seldom and coldly in comparison of other things? Follow thy own Heart Man, and observe what it daily runneth out after; and then judg whether it make not light of Christ.

We cannot perswade Men to one Hour's sober Consideration what they should do for an Interest in Christ, or in Thankfulness for his Love, and yet they will not believe that they make light of him.

2. Things that we highly value will be Matter of our Discourse: The Judgment and Heart will command the Tongue: Freely and delightfully will our Speech run after them: this also is a known Case.

Do not those then make light of Christ and Salvation, that shun the mention of his Name, unless it be in a vain or sinful Use? Those that love not the Company where Christ and Salvation is much talk'd of, but think it troublesom precise Discourse; that had rather hear some merry Jests, or idle Tales, or talk of their Riches or Business in the World: When you may follow them from Morning to Night, and scarce have a savoury Word of Christ, but perhaps some slight and weary mention of him sometimes; judg whether these make not light of Christ and Salvation, How seriously do they talk of the World, *Psal.* 144. 8, 11. and speak Vanity! but how heartlesly do they make mention of Christ and Salvation?

3. The things that we highly value, we would secure the Possession of, and therefore would take any convenient Course to have all Doubts and Fears about them well resolved. Do not those Men then make light of Christ and Salvation, that have lived 20 or 30 Years in Uncertainty whether they have any part in these or not, and yet never seek out for the right Resolution of their Doubts? Are all that hear me this Day certain they shall be saved? O that they were! O had you not made light of Salvation, you could not so easily bear such Doubtings of it; you could not rest till you had made it sure, or done your best to make it sure. Have you no Body to enquire of, that might help you in such a Work? Why you have Ministers that are purposely appointed to that Office. Have you gone to them, and told them the Doubtfulness of your Case, and asked their Help in the judging of your Condition? Alas, Ministers may sit in their Studies from one Year to another, before ten Persons among 1000 will come to them on such an Errand! Do not these make light of Christ and Salvation? When the Gospel pierceth the Heart indeed, they cry out, *Men and Brethren, what shall we do to be saved? Acts* 16. 30. and 9. 6. trembling and astonished *Paul* cries out, *Lord, what wilt thou have me to do?* And so did the convinced Jews to *Peter, Acts* 2. 37. But when hear we such Questions?

4. The things that we value, do *deeply affect* us, and some Motions will be in the Heart according to our Estimation of them. O Sirs, if Men made not light of these things, what working would there be in the Hearts of all our Hearers? what strange Affections would it raise in them to hear of the Matters of the World to come! How would their Hearts melt before the Power of the Gospel! what Sorrow would be wrought in the Discovery of their Sin! what Astonishment at the Consideration

ſideration of their Miſery! what unſpeakable Joy at the glad Tidings of Salvation by the Blood of Chriſt! what Reſolution would be raiſed in them upon the Diſcovery of their Duty! O what Hearers ſhould we have if it were not for this Sin! Whereas now we are liker to weary them, or preach them aſleep with Matters of this unſpeakable Moment. We talk to them of Chriſt and Salvation, till we make their Heads ake: Little would one think by their careleſs Carriage, that they heard and regarded what we ſaid, or thought we ſpoke at all to them.

5. Our Eſtimation of things will be ſeen in the diligence of our Endeavours. That which we highlieſt value, we ſhall think no pains too great to obtain. Do not thoſe Men then make light of Chriſt and Salvation, that think all too much that they do for them, that murmur at his Service, and think it too grievous for them to endure? that ask of his Service, as *Judas* of the Ointment, *What need this waſte? cannot Men be ſaved without ſo much ado? this is more ado than needs.* For the World they will labour all the Day, and all their Lives; but for Chriſt and Salvation they are afraid of doing too much. Let us preach to them as long as we will, we cannot bring them to reliſh or reſolve upon a Life of Holineſs. Follow them to their Houſes, and you ſhall not hear them read a Chapter, nor call upon God with their Families once a Day; nor will they allow him that one Day in ſeven which he hath ſeparated to his Service. But Pleaſure, or worldly Buſineſs, or Idleneſs muſt have a part. And many of them are ſo far hardened, as to reproach them that will not be as mad as themſelves. And is not Chriſt worth the ſeeking? Is not everlaſting Salvation worth more than all this? Doth not that Soul make light of all theſe, that thinks his Eaſe more worth than they? Let but common Senſe judg.

6. That which we moſt highly value, we think we cannot *buy too dear:* Chriſt and Salvation are freely given, and yet the moſt of Men go without them, becauſe

they

they cannot enjoy the World and them together. They are called but to part with that which would hinder them from Christ, and they will not do it. They are called but to give God his own, and to resign all to his Will, and let go the Profits and Pleasures of this World, when they must let go either Christ or them; and they will not. They think this too dear a Bargain, and say they cannot spare these things; they must hold their Credit with Men; they must look to their Estates, how shall they live else? they must have their Pleasure, whatsoever becomes of Christ and Salvation: As if they could live without Christ better than without these: as if they were afraid of being Losers by Christ, or could make a saving Match by losing their Souls to gain the World. Christ hath told us over and over, that if we will not forsake all for him, we cannot be his Disciples, *Luke* 14. 33. Far are these Men from forsaking all, and yet will needs think that they are his Disciples indeed.

7. That which Men highly esteem, they would *help their Friends to* as well as themselves. Do not those Men make light of Christ and Salvation, that can take so much care to leave their Children Portions in the World, and do so little to help them to Heaven? that provide outward Necessaries so carefully for their Families, but do so little to the saving of their Souls? Their neglected Children and Friends will witness, that either Christ, or their Childrens Souls, or both were made light of.

8. That which Men highly esteem, they will so diligently seek after, that you may see it in the *success*, if it be a Matter within their reach. You may see how many make light of Christ, by the little Knowledg they have of him, and the little Communion with him, and Communication from him; and the little, yea, none of his special Graces in them. Alas, how many Ministers can speak it to the Sorrow of their [illegible], that many of their People know almost non[illegible] [illegible]rist, though

they hear of him daily, nor know they what they must do to be saved! If we ask them an account of these things, they answer as if they understood not what we say to them, and tell us they are no Scholars, and therefore think they are excusable for their Ignorance. O if these Men had not made light of Christ and their Salvation, but had bestowed but half so much Pains to know and enjoy him, as they have done to understand the Matters of their Trades and Callings in the World, they would not have been so ignorant as they are: they make light of these things, and therefore will not be at the Pains to study or learn them. When Men that can learn the hardest Trade in a few Years, have not learned a Catechism, nor how to understand their Creed, under twenty or thirty Years Preaching, nor cannot abide to be questioned about such things; doth not this shew that they have slighted them in their Hearts? How will these Despisers of Christ and Salvation be able one Day to look him in the Face, and to give an account of these Neglects?

Thus much I have spoken in order to your Conviction. Do not some of your Consciences by this time smite you, and say, *I am the Man that have made light of my Salvation?* If they do not, it is because you make light of it still for all that is said to you. But because, if it be the Will of the Lord, I would fain have this damning Distemper cured, and am loth to leave you in such a desperate Condition, if I knew how to remedy it, I will give you some Considerations, which may move you, if you be Men of Reason and Understanding, to look better about you; and I beseech you weigh them, and make use of them as we go, and lay open your Hearts to the Work of Grace, and sadly bethink you what a Case you are in, if you prove such as make light of Christ.

Consider, 1. Thou makest light of him that made not light of thee who didst deserve it. Thou wast worthy of nothing but Contempt. As a Man, what art thou but a Worm to God? As a Sinner, thou art far viler than a Toad: yet Christ was so far from making light of thee and thy Happiness, that he came down into the Flesh, and lived a Life of Suffering, and offered himself a Sacrifice to the Justice which thou hadst provoked, that thy miserable Soul might have a Remedy. It is no less than Miracles of Love and Mercy that he hath shewed to us: and yet shall we slight them after all?

Angels admire them, whom they less concern, 1 *Pet.* 1. 12. and shall redeemed Sinners make light of them? What barbarous, yea devilish, yea worse than devilish Ingratitude is this? the Devils never had a Saviour offered them, but thou hast, and dost thou yet make light of him?

2. Consider the Work of Man's Salvation by Jesus Christ is the Master-piece of all the Works of God, wherein he would have his Love and Mercy to be magnified. As the Creation declareth his Goodness and Power, so doth Redemption his Goodness and Mercy; he hath contrived the very Frame of his Worship so, that it shall much consist in the magnifying of this Work; and after all this, will you make light of it? His Name is Wonderful, *Isa.* 9. 6. He did the Work that none could do, *John* 15. 24. Greater Love could none shew than this, *John* 15. 13. How great was the Evil and Misery that he delivered us from! the Good procured for us! all are Wonders from his Birth to his Ascension; from our new Birth to our Glorification, all are Wonders of matchless Mercy. And yet do you make light of them!

3. You make light of Matters of *greatest Excellency and Moment in the World*: you know not what it is that you slight; had you well known, you could not have done it. As Christ said to the Woman of *Samaria*, *John* 4. 10. hadst thou known who it is that speaketh to thee, thou wouldst have asked of him the Waters of Life: had they *known*, they would not have crucified the

the Lord of Glory, 1 *Cor.* 2. 8. So had you known what Christ is, you would not have made light of him; Had you been one Day in Heaven, and but seen what they possess, and seen also what miserable Souls must endure that are shut out, you would never sure have made so light of Christ again.

O Sirs, it is no Trifles or jesting Matters that the Gospel speaks of. I must needs profess to you, that when I have the most serious Thoughts of these things my self, I am ready to marvel that such amazing Matters do not overwhelm the Souls of Men: that the Greatness of the Subject doth not so overmatch our Understandings and Affections, as even to drive Men beside themselves, but that God hath always somewhat allayed it by the distance; much more that Men should be so blockish as to make light of them. O Lord, that Men did but know what everlasting Glory, and everlasting Torments are; would they then hear us as they do? would they read and think of these things as they do? I profess I have been ready to wonder when I have heard such weighty things delivered, how People can forbear crying out in the Congregation; much more, how they can rest till they have gone to their Ministers and learned what they should do to be saved, that this great Business might be put out of doubt. O that Heaven and Hell should work no more on Men! O that Everlastingness should work no more! O how can you forbear when you are alone, to think with your selves what it is to be everlastingly in Joy or in Torment! I wonder that such Thoughts do not break your Sleep; and that they come not in your mind when you are about your Labour! I wonder how you can almost do any thing else! How you can have any Quietness in your Minds! How you can eat, or drink, or rest, till you have got some Ground of everlasting Consolations! Is that a *Man* or a *Corps* that is not affected with Matters of this Moment? that can be readier to sleep, than to tremble, when he heareth how he must stand at the Bar of

God!

hard at hand. Truly Sirs, when I think of the Weight of the Matter, I wonder at the very beſt of God's Saints upon Earth, that they are no better, and do no more in ſo weighty a Caſe. I wonder at thoſe whom the World accounteth more holy than needs, and ſcorns for making too much ado; that they can put off Chriſt and their Souls with ſo little; that they pour not out their Souls in every Supplication; that they are not more taken up with God; that their Thoughts be not more ſerious in preparation for their Account. I wonder that they be not an hundred times more ſtrict in their Lives, and more laborious and unwearied in ſtriving for the Crown, than they are. And for my ſelf, as I am aſhamed of my dull and careleſs Heart, and of my ſlow and unprofitable Courſe of Life; ſo the Lord knows, I am aſhamed of every Sermon that I preach: when I think *what* I have been ſpeaking of, and *who* ſent me; and that Mens Salvation or Damnation is ſo much concerned in it. I am ready to tremble, leſt God ſhould judg me as a Slighter of his Truth, and the Souls of Men, and leſt in the beſt Sermon I ſhould be guilty of their Blood. Methinks we ſhould not ſpeak a Word to Men in Matters of ſuch Conſequence, without Tears, or the greateſt Earneſtneſs that poſſibly we can: were not we too much guilty of the Sin which we reprove, it would be ſo. Whether we are alone, or in Company, methinks our End, and ſuch an End, ſhould ſtill be in our Mind, and as before our Eyes; and we ſhould ſooner forget any thing, and ſet light by any thing, or by all things, than by this.

Conſider, 4. Who is it that ſends this weighty Meſſage to you? Is it not God himſelf? Shall the God of Heaven ſpeak, and Men make light of it? You would

would not slight the Voice of an Angel or a Prince.

5. *Whose* Salvation is it that you make light of? Is it not your own? Are you no more near or dear to your selves, than to make light of your *own* Happiness or Misery? Why Sirs, do you not care whether you be saved or damned? Is Self-love lost? Are you turned your own Enemies? As he that slighteth his Meat doth slight his Life; so if you slight Christ, whatsoever you may think, you will find it was your own Salvation that you slighted. Hear what he saith, *Prov.* 8. 36. *All they that hate me, love Death.*

6. Your Sin is greater, in that you profess to believe the Gospel which you make so light of. For a professed Infidel to do it, that believes not that ever Christ died, or rose again, or doth not believe that there is an Heaven or Hell, this were no such marvel; but for you that make it your Creed, and your very Religion, and call your selves Christians, and have been baptized into this Faith, and seemed to stand to it, this is the Wonder, and hath no Excuse. What! believe that you shall live in endless Joy or Torment, and yet make no more of it, to escape Torment, and obtain that Joy. What! believe that God will shortly judg you, and yet make no more Preparation for it. Either say plainly, *I am no Christian, I do not believe these wonderful things, I will believe nothing but what I see*; or else let your Hearts be affected with your Belief, and live as you say you do believe. What do you think when you repeat the Creed, and mention Christ's Judgment, and everlasting Life?

7. What are these things you set so much by, as to prefer them before Christ, and the saving of your Souls? Have you found a better Friend, a greater and surer Happiness than this? Good Lord! what Dung is it that Men make so much of, while they set so light by everlasting Glory! What Toys are they that they are daily taken up with, while Matters of Life and Death are neglected! Why Sirs, if you had every one a Kingdom in your Hopes, what were it in comparison of the ever-

lasting Kingdom? I cannot but look upon all the Glory and Dignity of this World, Lands and Lordships, Crowns and Kingdoms, even as on some brainsick beggarly Fellow, that borroweth fine Clothes, and plays the Part of a King or a Lord for an Hour on a Stage, and then comes down, and the Sport is ended, and they are Beggars again. Were it not for God's Interest in the Authority of Magistrates, or for the Service they might do him, I should judg no better of them. For as to their own Glory, it is but a Smoak: what matter is it whether you live poor or rich, unless it were a greater Matter to *die* rich than it is? You know well enough that Death levels all: what Matter is it at Judgment, whether you be to answer for the Life of a rich Man, or a poor Man? Is *Dives* then any better than *Lazarus*? O that Men knew what a poor deceiving Shadow they grasp at, while they let go the everlasting Substance! The strongest and richest, and most voluptuous Sinners, do but lay in fuel for their Sorrows, while they think they are gathering together a Treasure. Alas, they are asleep, and dream that they are happy; but when they awake, what a Change will they find! Their Crown is made of Thorns: their Pleasure hath such a Sting as will stick in the Heart through all Eternity, except unfeigned Repentance do prevent it. O how sadly will these Wretches be convinced ere long what a foolish Bargain they made in selling Christ and their Salvation for these Trifles! Let your Farms and Merchandize then save you if they can, and do that for you that Christ would have done. Cry then to thy *Baal* to save thee. O what Thoughts have Drunkards and Adulterers, *&c.* of Christ, that will not part with the basest Lust for him! For a piece of Bread, saith *Solomon*, such Men do transgress, *Prov.* 28. 21.

8. To set so light by Christ and Salvation is a certain Mark that thou hast no part in them, and if thou so continue, that Christ will set *as light* by thee: those that honour him he will honour, and those that despise him

nd submit to him here. Then who will
er by thy Contempt? O what a thing will
or miserable Soul to cry to Christ for Help
Extremity, and to hear so sad an Answer
i didst set light by me and my Law in the
rosperity, and I will now set as light by
Adversity. Read *Prov.* 1. 24 to the end.
Esau, didst sell thy Birth-right for a Mess of
t then find no Place for Repentance, though
with Tears, *Heb.* 12. 17. Do you think
ed his Blood to save them that continue to
it? and to save them that value a Cup
a Lust, before his Salvation? I tell you
you set so light by Christ and Salvation, *God*
: He will not give them on such Terms
e valueth the Blood of his Son, and the
Glory; and he will make *you* value them,
ave them. Nay, this will be thy Condem-
leaveth no Remedy. All the World cannot
it sets light by Christ, *Heb.* 2. 3. *Luke* 14.
of them shall taste of his Supper, *Mat.* 10.
n you blame him to deny you what you
of your selves. Can you find fault if you
alvation which you slighted?
ne is near when Christ and Salvation will
light of, as now they are. When God hath
careless Souls out of their Bodies, and you
for all your Sins in your own Name; O
ould you give for a Saviour! when a thousand
brought in against you, and none to relieve
ou will consider, *O Christ would now have
me and the Wrath of God: had I not despised
have answered all.* When you see the World

hath left you, and your Companions in Sin have deceived themselves and you, and all your merry Day's are gone; then what would you give for that Christ and Salvation that now you account not worth your Labour? Do you think, when you see the Judgment set, and you are doomed to everlasting Perdition for your Wickedness, that you should then make as light of Christ as now? Why will you not judg now, as you know you shall judg then? Will he then be worth ten thousand Worlds, and is he not now worth your highest Estimation, and dearest Affection?

10. God will not only deny thee that Salvation thou madest light of, but he will take from thee all that which thou didst value before it: He that most highly esteems Christ, shall have him and the Creatures so far as they are good here, and him without the Creature hereafter, because the Creature is not useful; and he that sets more by the Creature than by Christ, shall have some of the Creature without Christ here, and neither Christ nor it hereafter.

So much of these Considerations, which may shew the true Face of this heinous Sin.

What think you now, Friends, of this Business? Do you not see by this time what a Case that Soul is in that maketh light of Christ and Salvation? What need then is there that you should take heed lest this should prove your own Case? The Lord knows it is too common a Case. Whoever is found guilty at the last of this Sin, it were better for that Man he had never been born. It were better for him he had been a *Turk* or *Indian*, that never had heard the Name of a Saviour, and that never had Salvation offered to him: For such Men have no cloak for their Sin, *John* 15. 22. Besides all the rest of their Sins, they have this killing Sin to answer for, which will undo them. And this will aggravate their Misery, *That* Christ whom they set light by, must be their Judg, and for *this* Sin will he judg them. O that such would now consider how they will answer that Question

that

that Christ puts to their Predecessors, *Matth.* 23. 33. *How will ye escape the Damnation of Hell?* or *Heb.* 2. 3. *How shall we escape if we neglect so great Salvation?* Can you escape without a Christ? or will a despised Christ save you then? If he be accursed that sets light by Father or Mother, *Deut.* 27. 16. what then is he that sets light by Christ? It was the heinous Sin of the Jews, that among them were found such as set light by Father and Mother, *Ezek.* 22. 7. but among us, Men slight the Father of Spirits. In the Name of God, Brethren, I beseech you to consider how you will then bear his Anger which you now make light of? You that cannot make light of a little Sickness or Want, or of natural Death, no not of a Tooth-ach, but groan as if you were undone, how will you then make light of the Fury of the Lord, which will burn against the Contemners of his Grace? Doth it not behove you beforehand to think of these things?

Hitherto I have been convincing you of the Evil of the Sin, and the Danger that followeth: I come now to know your Resolution for the time to come. What say you? Do you mean to set as light by Christ and Salvation as hitherto you have done? and to be the same Men after all this? I hope not. O let not your Ministers that would fain save you, be brought in as Witnesses against you to condemn you. At least, I beseech you put not this upon me. Why Sirs, if the Lord shall say to us at Judgment, Did you never tell these Men what Christ did for their Souls, and what need they had of him, and how nearly it did concern them to look to their Salvation, that they made not light of it? we must needs say the Truth: Yea Lord, we told them of it as plainly as we could; we would have gone on our Knees to them, if we had thought it would have prevailed; we did intreat them as earnestly as we could to consider these things: they heard of these things every day; but alas, we could never get 'em to their Hearts: they gave us the hearing, but they made light of all that we could say to them.

O sad will it prove on your side, if you force us to such an Answer as this.

But if the Lord do move the Hearts of any of you, and you resolve to make light of Christ no more: Or if any of you say, We do not make light of him; let me tell you here in the Conclusion, what you must do, or else you shall be judged as Slighters of Christ and Salvation.

And first, I will tell you what will not serve the turn.

1. You may have a notional Knowledg of Christ, and the Necessity of his Blood, and of the Excellency of Salvation, and yet perish as Neglecters of him. This is too common among profest Christians. You may say all that other Men do of him. What Gospel-Passages had *Balaam?* Jesus I know, and *Paul* I know, the very Devils could say, who believe and tremble, *Jam.* 2. 19.

2. You may weep at the History of his Passion, when you read how he was used by the Jews; and yet make light of him, and perish for so doing.

3. You may come desirously to his Word and Ordinances. *Herod* heard gladly; so do many that yet must perish as Neglecters of Salvation.

4. You may in a fit of Fear have strong Desires after a Christ to ease you, and to save you from God's Wrath, as *Saul* had of *David* to play before him; and yet you may perish for making light of Christ.

5. You may obey him in many things, so far as will not ruine you in the World, and escape much of the Pollutions of the World by his Knowledg; and yet neglect him.

6. You may suffer and lose much for him, so far as leaveth you an earthly Felicity; as *Ananias*, the young Man. Some Parcels of their Pleasures and Profits many will part with in Hope of Salvation, that shall perish everlastingly, for valuing it no more.

be judged as Contemners of him: Christ
ll that justify themselves.
y be zealous Preachers of Christ and Sal-
eprove others for this neglect, and lament
World in the like Expression as I have
; and yet if you or I have no better Evi-
e our hearty Esteem of Christ and Salva-
undone for all this.

Brethren, what will *not* serve the turn;
hear what Persons you *must* be if you would
ned as Slighters of Christ? O search whe-
is with your Souls or no.
steem of Christ and Salvation, must be
your Esteem of all the Honours, Profits
of this World, or else you slight him:
accounted sincere, nor accepted to your
hink not this hard, when there is no Com-
Matters esteemed. To esteem the great-
Earth before Christ and everlasting Glory,
Folly, and Wrong to Christ, than to e-
before your Prince, would be Folly in you,
ng to him. Scripture is plain in this,
7. *He that loveth Father or Mother, Wife,*
se, Land, or his own Life more than me, is not
and cannot be my Disciple, as *Luke* 14. 26.
ust manifest this Esteem of Christ and Sal-
ur daily Endeavours and seeking after him,
ng with any thing that he shall require of
is a Spirit, and will not take an hypocriti-
n instead of the Heart and spiritual Service
mmandeth. He will have the Heart or no-
the chief Room in the Heart too. These

H If

If you say that you do not make light of Christ, or will not hereafter, let me try you in these few Particulars, whether indeed you mean as you say, and do not dissemble.

1. Will you for the time to come make Christ and Salvation the chiefest Matter of your Care and Study? Thrust them not out of your Thoughts, as a needless or unprofitable Subject; nor allow it only some running slight Thoughts, which will not affect you. But will you make it your Business once a Day to bethink you soberly when you are alone, what Christ hath done for you; and what he will do if you do not make light of it; and what it is to be everlastingly happy or miserable? and what all things in this World are in comparison of your Salvation? and how they will shortly leave you? and what mind you will be then of, and how you will esteem them? Will you promise me now and then to make it your Business to withdraw your selves from the World, and set your selves to such Considerations as these? If you will not, are not you Slighters of Christ and Salvation, that will not be perswaded soberly to think on them? This is my first Question to put you to the Trial, whether you will value Christ or not.

2. Will you for the time to come, set more by the Word of God, which contains the Discovery of these excellent things, and is your Charter for Salvation, and your Guide thereunto? You cannot set by Christ, but you must set by his Word: Therefore the Despisers of it are threatned with Destruction, *Prov.* 13. 13. Will you therefore attend to the publick preaching of this Word? will you read it daily? will you resolve to obey it whatever it may cost you? If you will not do this, but make light of the Word of God, you shall be judged such as make light of Christ and Salvation, whatever you may fondly promise to your selves.

the Necessity of *your* Souls that God hath set them in his Church; that they may be as Physicians under Christ, or his Apothecaries to apply his Remedies to your spiritual Diseases, not only in publick, but also in private: That you may have some to go to for the resolving of your Doubts, and for your Instruction where you are ignorant, and for the help of their Exhortations and Prayers. Will you use hereafter to go to your Ministers privately, and solicite them for Advice? and if you have not such of your own as are fit, get Advice from others; and ask them *What you shall do to be saved? how to prepare for Death and Judgment?* and will you obey the Word of God in their Mouths? If you will not do this much, nor so much as enquire of those that should teach you, nor use the Means which Christ hath established in his Church for your help, your own Consciences shall one Day witness, that you were such as made light of Christ and Salvation. If any of you doubt whether it be your Duty thus to ask Counsel of your Teachers, as sick Men do of their Physicians, let your own Necessities resolve you; let God's express Word resolve you: see what is said of the Priests of the Lord, even before Christ's coming, when much of their Work did lie in Ceremonials; *Mal.* 2. 5, 6. *My Covenant was with him of Life and Peace: and I gave them to him* (to *Levi*) *for the fear wherewith he feared me, and was afraid before my Name. The Law of Truth was in his Mouth, and Iniquity was not found in his Lips; he walked with me in Peace and Equity, and did turn many away from Iniquity. For the Priests Lips should keep Knowledg, and they should seek the Law at his Mouth: for he is the Messenger of the Lord of Hosts.*

Nay, you must not only enquire, and submit to their Advice, but also to their just Reprehensions and Church-Censures: And without proud Repining submit to the Discipline of Christ in their Hands, if it shall be used in the Congregations whereof you are Members.

4. Will you for the time to come make Conscience of daily and earnest Prayer to God, that you may have a Part in Christ and Salvation? do not go out of Doors till you have breathed out these Desires to God; do not lie down to rest till you have breathed out these Desires: say not, God knoweth my Necessity without so often praying; for though he do, yet he will have you to know them and feel them, and exercise your Desires, and all the Graces of his Spirit in these Duties: It is he that hath commanded to pray continually, though he know your Needs without, 1 *Thess.* 5. 17. Christ himself spent whole Nights in Prayer, and encourageth us to this Course, *Luke* 18.1. If you will not be perswaded to this much, how can you say that you make not light of Christ and Salvation?

5. Will you for the time to come resolvedly cast away your known Sins at the Command of Christ? If you have been proud or contentious, or malicious and revengeful, be so no more. If you have been Adulterers, or Swearers, or Cursers, be so no more. You cannot hold these, and yet set by Christ and Salvation.

What say you? Are you resolved to let them go? If not, when you know 'tis the Will of Christ, and he hath told you such shall not enter into his Kingdom, do not you make light of him?

6. Will you for the time to come serve God in the *dearest* as well as the *cheapest* Part of his Service; not only with your Tongues, but with your Purses and your Deeds? shall the Poor find that you set more by Christ than this World? shall it appear in any good Uses that

God

Terms too dear, you make light of Chri
judged accordingly.

7. Will you for the time to come mak
things that tend to your Salvation; and ta
that God offereth you, and gladly make
Ordinances? Attend upon his ſtrengtheni
ſpend the Lord's own Day in theſe holy
Inſtruct your Children and Servants in
Deut. 6. 6, 7. get into good Company
Faces Heaven-ward, and will teach you
help you thither: and take heed of th
wicked Scorners, or fooliſh, voluptuous
or any that would hinder you in this Wo
do theſe things? Or will you ſhew that yo
of Chriſt by neglecting them?

8. Will you do all this with Delight
Toil, but as your Pleaſure? and take it fo
Honour that you may be Chriſt's Diſci
be *admitted* to ſerve and worſhip him; an
holy Confidence in the ſufficiency of th
which you may have Pardon of all you
right to the Inheritance of the Saints in
will do theſe things ſincerely, you will
ſet by Chriſt and Salvation; elſe not.

Dearly Beloved in the Lord, I have
Work which I came upon; what Effect
have upon your Hearts, I know not, nor
in my Power to accomplish that which m
for you. Were it the Lord's Will tha
my wiſh herein, the Words that you
heard ſhould ſo ſtick by you, that the

be awakened by them, and none of you should perish by the slighting of your Salvation. I cannot now follow you to your several Habitations, to apply the Word to your particular Necessities: but O that I could make every Man's *Conscience* a Preacher to himself, that *it* might do it, which is ever with you; that the next time you go prayerless to Bed, or about your Business, Conscience might cry out, *Dost thou set no more by Christ and by Salvation?* that the next time you are tempted to think hardly of an holy and diligent Life, (I will not say to deride it as *more ado than needs*) Conscience might cry out to thee, *Dost thou set so light by Christ and thy Salvation?* that the next time you are ready to rush upon known Sin, and to please your fleshly Desires against the Command of God, Conscience might cry out, *Is Christ and Salvation no more worth, than to cast them away, or venture them for thy Lusts?* that when you are following the World with your most eager Desires, forgetting the World to come and the Change that is a little before you, Conscience might cry out to you, *Is Christ and Salvation no more worth than so?* That when you are next spending the Lord's Day in Idleness or vain Sports, Conscience might tell you what you are doing. In a Word, that in all your Neglects of Duty, your sticking at the supposed Labour or Cost of a godly Life, yea in all your cold and lazy Prayers and Performances, Conscience might tell you how unsutable such Endeavours are to the Reward; and that Christ and Salvation should not be so slighted. I will say no more but this at this time, it is a thousand Pities that when God hath provided a Saviour for the World, and when Christ hath suffered so much for their Sins, and made so full a Satisfaction to Justice, and purchased so glorious a Kingdom for his Saints, and all this is offered so freely to Sinners, to lost unworthy Sinners, even for nothing, that yet so many Millions should everlastingly perish because they *make light*

t[illegible]

[illegible]r *Saviour and Salvation, and prefer the vain World and* *heir Lusts before them.* I have delivered my Message; he Lord open your Hearts to receive it: I have perswa-d you with the *Word* of Truth and Soberness; the rd perswade you more effectually, or else all this is [illegible]

FINIS.

www.ingramcontent.com/pod-product-compliance
Lightning Source LLC
Chambersburg PA
CBHW030555270326
41927CB00007B/933

* 9 7 8 3 3 3 7 2 8 9 9 5 9 *